THE FASHION DESIGNER'S HANDBOOK

AND KIT

Learn to Sew and Become a Designer in 33 Fabulous Projects

BY MARJORIE GALEN

WORKMAN PUBLISHING · NEW YORK

To my parents, Robert and Judith Galen

Library of Congress Cataloging-in-Publication Data is available.

ISBN 978-0-7611-5479-2

Book design by Rae Ann Spitzenberger
Illustrations by Jason Lee
Photography by Marjorie Galen
Photo Stylists: Caitlin Betsy Bell, Diana Green, Ellie Kitman
Fashion Drawings and Collages Courtesy of Ellie Kitman, Emma Tung, Allison Gross

Barbie Doll is a registered trademark of Mattel.

Tyvek is a registered trademark of DuPont. Sindy is the registered trademark used under license from Pedigree Dolls and Toys Limited.

Workman books are available at special discounts when purchased in bulk for premiums and sales promotions as well as for fund-raising or educational use. Special editions or book excerpts also can be created to specification. For details, contact the Special Sales Director at the address below or send an e-mail to specialmarkets@workman.com.

WORKMAN PUBLISHING COMPANY, INC.
225 Varick Street
New York, NY 10014-4381
www.workman.com

Printed in China
First printing October 2011

10 9 8 7 6 5 4 3 2 1

- -

My thanks to ...

My editors Ruth Sullivan and Margot Herrera, designers Janet Vicario and Rae Ann Spitzenberger, and everyone at Workman, my children Ike and Ellie Kitman, my sister Elizabeth Greene and family, my pattern tester Sophia Carroll, Dana Stangel-Plowe, as well as Glenn Morrow, Suzanna Frosch, Blake Tovin, Diana Green, Chris Carroll, Liz Mechem, Caitlin Betsy Bell, Richard Killeaney, Denyse Schmidt, Martha Flach Wilkie, Robin Goldwasser, Jerry Reynolds and Rachel Pym at Pedigree Group, Patricia McDonough, and all the adorable models: Lucy, Emma, and Caroline Plowe, Jamila Wilkinson, Sophia and Lucinda Carroll, Alexa Schilero, and Isabel Wecht.

Contents

Tube Dress

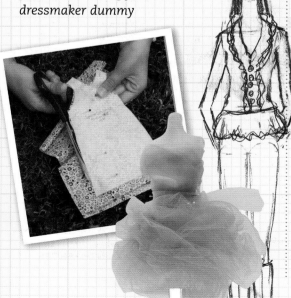

Mod Mini
1-2-3 Skirt

Princess
Party Dress

Messenger Bag

Summer
Shift Dress
from page 66

Trapezoid
T-Skirt

Introduction

I remember being 12 years old, walking down the street near my house, wearing my brand-new purple velour bell-bottom pants with square patch pockets in front. A necklace of colorful love beads—real love beads direct from hippies in New York City's Washington Square Park—bounced against my chest. I'm sure I didn't look as cool as I felt, but I remember feeling like I owned the place. Since that day, I've loved other items of clothing, but I've never been as sure about one as I was about those purple bell-bottoms.

* * *

How about you? Do you have a favorite outfit that reflects the real you? Do you mix and match your tops and bottoms and add accessories until you get it just right? Did you know that when you do, you're acting like a fashion designer? Just like you pick and choose different clothes from your closet, real fashion designers pick and choose from their mental library of silhouettes, color combinations, fabrics, patterns, and textures to make up their new collections.

When you're getting dressed, do you imagine what if . . . what if this skirt was fuller, this top more cropped, maybe this skirt should have a ruffle? If you answered yes, this book is a great place to begin. In *The Fashion Designer's Handbook,* you'll learn all you need to know to design and sew doll-sized clothes, and then, when you've gotten the hang of it, to begin making clothes for yourself!

The Fashion Designer's Handbook contains patterns and instructions to make 33 adorable projects for a Barbie-sized doll, from shimmery party dresses to miniskirts and doll-sized blue jeans, plus fun accessories and variations so you can make the changes *you* want.

I love, love, love to sew, but the fun thing about writing this book has been dressing all the dolls. As a kid, I never had a Barbie doll. I know it sounds impossible that a girl could grow up in the United States post-Barbie (she was introduced in 1959) and not have one single Barbie, but it's true. I was a tomboy and working on the book showed me what I missed by being a girl who played baseball instead of dolls.

Sixty dolls—all in different outfits—filled my mantel.

To get started, I went on eBay and bought as many 11½-inch fashion dolls (that's what they call Barbie-sized dolls) as I could find. It seems that collectors want the dolls to be dressed, but I didn't, so they were inexpensive, and I bought a lot of them. Once they arrived, I started making tiny pleated kilts, appliquéd jackets, T-shirt dresses, and pink silk ball gowns, and dressing up the dolls. Every day I sewed something new and different, dressed up a doll or two, and posed them on my fireplace mantel. I changed the outfits slightly each time, trying out different fabrics, reshaping, adding ruffles, trim, and embroidery. Finally

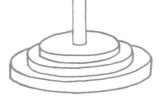

the fireplace mantel was full of dolls—there must have been 60 of them up there—and I knew I was ready to write this book. When I was a girl, I would have loved to have a book like this because it would have shown me that even though it looks difficult to design and sew an outfit, it's really very easy. So, here is a guide to help you find your design voice and then make your dreams into dresses or pants . . . or whatever fun fashions you can think up.

CHAPTER 1

So You Want to Be a Fashion Designer?

Remember when you decided it was time for you, not your mother, to pick out your clothes? You knew what you wanted to wear, what looked good on you, and what colors you liked; and you knew that no one else could get it right. You insisted on picking out your clothes because you wanted to dress your own way. I understand; I was the same way, and so is my daughter.

* * *

When I was a little girl, my grandmother's closet was a magical place, full of sophisticated evening dresses, multicolored silk scarves, lacy slips, tweed coats, bits of fur, and impossibly tall high heels. I couldn't imagine when and where my grandmother could possibly wear these movie-star clothes. Every chance we got, my sister and I would play dress-up in her closet.

Here we were, two little girls in messy pigtails, wearing cocktail dresses that came down to our ankles, wrapped in scarves and fur stoles, with bright red lipstick smeared across the general area of our lips, and tottering on high heels.

More than fun, playing dress-up was good practice. When you mix and match and try things on you're developing a sense of style; and that's the first step to becoming a fashion designer.

In your kit you'll find a miniature (doll-sized) dress form. Just like a real designer, you can wrap fabric around the dress form, tuck it, or pin it, add trim and ties, and create new designs of your own. It's like playing dress-up, but doll-sized.

How to Think Like a Designer in 4 Easy Steps

Maybe you dream of being a fashion designer like on *Project Runway*, or maybe you just want to have fun making things for your dolls or yourself. Either way, this book will help you get started. But first things first, you need to learn to think like a designer.

Step 1
STYLE RULES!

Ever had a bad clothing day? One of those days when you get out of bed and no matter how many outfits you try on, you just can't figure out what to wear? What were you thinking as you searched your closet, scanning the options? Did you wonder if your outfit looked good? Or maybe it was more like you were worrying about whether the outfit fit—in more ways than one. Did it express your personal style or mood that day? Did it say something about you? Was it appropriate for wherever you were going— to school, the movies, or a party?

Whether we like it or not, the clothes we wear send a message. A tailored dress for a girl or a dark suit for a boy tells people you take life seriously or, at least, that you take life seriously at that moment. A flouncy skirt and ballet flats might say you're a girl who likes a bit of fun or, at least, that you're feeling playful and girly that day. Most people, consciously or subconsciously, decide on a style and stick with it. Yes, even kids! Just like adults, many kids have their own uniform of sorts; whether it's jeans and a T-shirt, exclusively dresses, or everything in pink. They know what they like and what looks good on them, and every day is another variation on the theme.

Other kids rarely wear the same thing twice, mixing and matching to surprise themselves, and everyone else, with new combinations every day. Think about your friends— even if you couldn't see their faces, I bet you could recognize them by their clothing choices!

You can experiment and express your inner fashionista every morning when you get dressed. Even if you don't make your own clothes, you still make choices about how you put outfits together. The individual touches—or personal flair—create a look that is truly your own. Style is not about being able to afford

the latest designer fashion. Style is something else entirely, something more. In fact, you can have style on practically no money at all!

In the 1960s, street styles began to influence the fashion designers. And it still does. Fashion companies actually hire trend scouts to go around to the cool neighborhoods of the world—New York, London, Tokyo, you name it—and report back on what the "kids" are wearing. So when some hipster decides to wear baggy pants, or poufy skirts, or only step out in glittery thrift-store clothes, it's only a matter of weeks before that same style is copied by fashion companies, is mass-produced, and appears in the shop windows.

Look at kids on the street and see what they're wearing, and how they're wearing it. People all around you are doing interesting things with clothing; pay attention to what you like. Get inspired by looking at fashion magazines and catalogs; pick out a piece of clothing, and imagine how you'd like to change it. You can trace it, or copy it, or just cut it out; and then draw your changes right on top.

Step 2
GET INSPIRED

Where do designers (you) get ideas? Creative ideas in fashion, as in any other field, don't come out of nowhere. Open your eyes and look around. Every dress you admire, every painting you look at, every movie you see, every walk in the park—everything you experience can be a source of inspiration for creating your own

look. Bring along your sketchbook or carry a pocket-sized digital camera and record everything you see and like.

Keep a style file. All designers do it. Get a big bulletin board, then cut out interesting fashion from magazines and catalogs and pin them up. Put up swatches of fabric, postcards of places you'd like to visit, photographs of forests and stormy skies, color combinations you love—anything that inspires you. Keep a folder on your desk, or on your computer, if you don't have room for a bulletin board. Look at the ideas on page 6 and go out and get inspired!

Bulletin board with swatches

Step 3
LEARN TO SKETCH

They say a picture's worth a thousand words. It's one thing to describe your idea for a new dress or skirt, and another to draw a picture to show what you mean. Start out by looking at fashion illustrations in books and by studying photographs of models from magazines. You might begin by copying or tracing the models and the illustrations. (You'll notice that female models are much taller and skinnier than anyone you know.) And of course, you can always copy or trace the figures we've included on pages 114–117 to sketch your outfits on.

In fashion school you'll learn how to sketch a figure. But why not try your hand at it now by following the six steps, below.

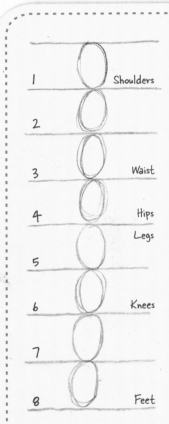

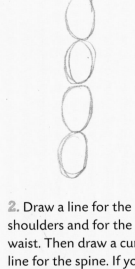

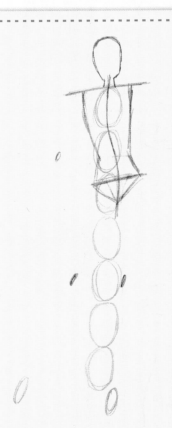

1. Begin by sketching eight ovals on top of each other. See where the shoulders, waist, hips, and legs fall.

2. Draw a line for the shoulders and for the waist. Then draw a curved line for the spine. If your pose is cocky, the shoulders will be slanted and the spine curvier.

3. Block in the upper body and hips. Make dots for the elbows (at waist), knees (six heads down), and feet. The position of the knees and feet are important for the stance and attitude.

The first thing to learn is proportion. The human figure is about eight head-lengths high, using the head as the unit of measure. (See drawing in step 1 for where waist, legs, knees, etc., fall.) It might surprise you that the legs are about half of the body, especially on fashion models where the legs are exaggeratedly long (and skinny).

Once you get the proportions and basic anatomy right, try different poses by varying the leg, feet, and arm positions.

4. Make oval shapes to connect the dots, from the end of the shoulder to the elbow, and then to the hand. Then connect the dots from hips to knees and knees to feet.

5. Give shape to the ovals; have the legs come in at the knee and curve out for the calf muscle. Leave the hands and feet sketchy. Erase the original ovals.

6. Using tracing paper, place it over your model and sketch your design ideas. You might want to draw in different hairstyles for different outfits.

Step 4
STUDY THE PAST

If you're interested in making a career in fashion, you're going to have to learn about fashion history.

Looking at clothes from the past will train your eye. A style from 25, 50, or even 100 years ago often influences the clothing you'll see on the runway next year. And

"New Look" of the '50s

designers keep recycling those looks. The straight, short flapper dresses of the 1920s came back as mod minidresses in the 1960s, and then as New Wave in the 1980s.

Sometimes when fashion designers talk about the past, they talk about silhouettes. The silhouette of a garment is the shape it makes when it's worn, and it is one way to date a garment. For example, the 1950s silhouette was

like an hourglass with a small waist and full skirt. By the 1960s, women wore straight suits with short jackets. That shape is more like a column or a T.

Different silhouettes and styles pop up again and again, referencing the past, and influencing the future. So if those nipped-in waists and crinolines you see in paintings from the 1800s look weird, just wait; maybe they'll be next year's big thing.

Where to Get Inspiration

Shop, Don't Drop
Go shopping, but just to look. Think about shapes and textures of fabrics, see what different colors do when they're next to each other. Bring your camera or sketchbook and record what you see. Say it's for a school assignment.

Saturday in the Park
Forms and colors in nature inspire designers: a bright green leaf is the basis for a spring collection; zebra stripes give rise to a black-and-white theme. And while you're out, snap shots of any people whose outfits strike your fancy.

The Big (and Small) Screen
Old movies and TV shows are the best ways to check out vintage style, and you'll get to know the famous style icons—actresses like Audrey Hepburn, Katharine Hepburn, Grace Kelly, or Marilyn Monroe—who still reign supreme in designers' minds.

Don't forget the music scene's huge influence on the fashion of the day—from Michael Jackson and Madonna to P. Diddy, Gwen Stefani, Miley Cyrus, Beyoncé, and Lady Gaga. Check out old and new performances and music pix online.

Lady Gaga at Grammy Awards

Research Online
Scroll around museum websites like the Metropolitan Museum's Costume Institute in New York City, or the Smithsonian Museum in Washington, D.C.

CHAPTER 2

Let's Talk About Fabric and Color

THREE BASIC TYPES OF FABRIC

Unless you're a paper doll, it's hard to get dressed without fabric. The kind of fabric affects the way clothes fit, hang, move, look, wear, feel on your skin, and swish when you walk. Learning how they're made and how they behave is an important first step in choosing fabrics for your projects.

WOVEN

Woven fabrics are made of horizontal and vertical yarns that are crisscrossed on a machine called a loom. The process is the same as when you wove pot holders at summer camp.

KNITTED

You might think only sweaters are knitted fabric, but T-shirt fabric (cotton jersey) is knitted too. It is made on machines that interconnect loops of thread or yarn. Knitted fabrics stretch, take on the form of the body, and don't unravel easily when cut.

NONWOVEN

Nonwoven fabrics are made by using heat or chemicals and friction to bind the fibers together. Wool felt doesn't unravel when cut. To make your own wool felt, see page 83.

The Fibers and How They Fall

WOOL

Wool, which comes from sheep, keeps you warm, but it also breathes. It's good for cold weather wear because it absorbs about 30 percent of its weight in moisture before it feels damp.

SYNTHETICS

Tulle, spandex, polyester, nylon, Polarfleece, and Kevlar are all man-made synthetic fabrics. Synthetic fibers are popular and practical.

COTTON

Cotton comes from the seedpod of a cotton plant, and is used to make many different woven fabrics, like denim, quilting cotton, and canvas. Cotton is also knitted and made into cotton jersey for T-shirts and sweatshirts. Cotton dries quickly and is great to wear in the summer.

SILK

Silk fibers come from the cocoon of the silkworm. The beauty of silk is the way it holds color. Silk drapes and folds gracefully. Try it on the dummy and see.

LINEN

Linen comes from the stalk of the flax plant, and is spun into thread and woven into fabric. Linen fabric is two times stronger than cotton, and it tends to wrinkle.

Color

little color info really helps in pulling an outfit together. Look around you at school and you'll see that mostly the palette is bright—T-shirts with colorful printed slogans, patterned skirts, multicolored tights—a riot of color and fun all mixed and matched into one-of-a-kind styles.

PRIMARY COLORS

Everywhere there's light there's color. This is because light is made up of many colors—some we can see, some we can't. The three basic, or primary, colors are red, yellow, and blue. By mixing the primary colors, you can create all the other colors of the rainbow. Mix the three primary colors together and you get brown.

SECONDARY COLORS

Secondary colors are made by mixing together two primary colors. The secondary colors are orange, green, and violet. They appear between the primary colors on the color wheel.

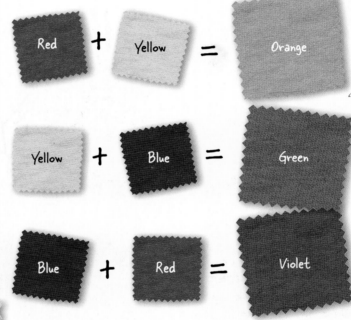

COLOR WHEEL

The colors are arranged in the order of the colors of the spectrum of light, also known as the colors of the rainbow.

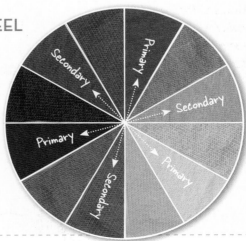

COMPLEMENTARY COLORS

Each primary color has a special relationship with the secondary color made by mixing the other two primary colors. These colors are called complementary and they make each other pop when worn together. Choose complementary colors when you want an outfit that makes some "noise." The complementary colors are:

Yellow & Violet

Red & Green

Blue & Orange

ANALOGOUS COLORS

More harmonious outfits can be made by using what are called analogous colors, that is, any three colors next to one another on the color wheel, for example, yellow, yellow-green, and green.

A quiet outfit of blues and purples.

Strong yellow and green blend together.

HAVE FUN!

Now that you know about color theory, forget all about it and just have fun experimenting. Find out what colors you like together—and look good on you. Above all, don't be afraid to trust your judgment. If you think it looks good, it probably does!

Building Your Fabric Collection

There's probably lots of fabric around your house . . . old T-shirts, the dress your baby sister has outgrown, and even paper towels (see page 19), or those shiny fabriclike overnight mail envelopes (made from a material called Tyvek).

If you know anyone who sews (maybe a friend's parent or older sibling), ask if they have any scraps—most people who sew are happy to encourage a beginner! Part of the fun of making these doll clothes is that very small pieces of fabric make amazing-looking outfits.

When you shop for fabric at a store, you'll discover that it is sold by the yard, which is 36 inches long, and in a variety of widths. Most fabric

Antique lunchbox used to store fabric.

stores will sell you smaller pieces, a ¼ or even ⅛ of a yard. Quilting stores are great places to find colorful printed cotton fabrics; the precut fat quarters you'll find there are enough for most projects in this book. I buy fabric I like, even if I don't necessarily know what I'm going to do with it. Some people shop with a specific garment in mind, which is a good idea when you're making clothes for people and need several yards of fabric.

Before taking a trip to the fabric store, flip through the projects in *The Fashion Designer's Handbook* so you'll have some favorites in mind; then pick out a few fabrics you like, buy small pieces, and start your own collection.

My daughter, Ellie, chooses a Liberty floral at Purl Soho.

CHAPTER 3

Tools & Patterns

HOW TO USE THIS BOOK

Fold it, pin it, cut it, sew it. Sounds simple, right? Well, that's really all you need to know to make anything in this book. And we'll teach you those steps in these next few pages. Every project has a pattern and instructions telling you how to make clothes and dress your dolls in style. In your own style, that is. You choose the fabric, you pick the colors, you modify the patterns to make what you want, and you combine tops and bottoms until the outfit perfectly suits your taste . . . you're the designer here! You accessorize and add whatever trim is fun— like ribbons, appliqué, and embroidery.

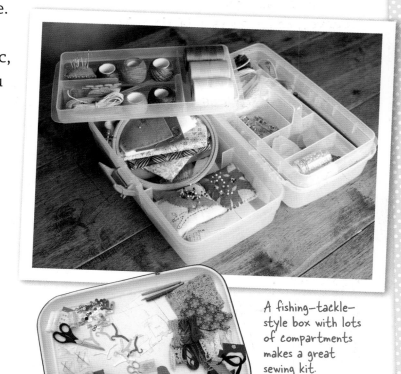

A fishing-tackle-style box with lots of compartments makes a great sewing kit.

Tools of the Rag Trade

There are really only three things you absolutely need to get started—scissors, needle, and thread. But the other things listed here are called for in some of the projects. All of them can be found around your house or at a sewing or craft store.

THE THREE BASICS

1. SCISSORS

Sharp fabric scissors cut cloth smoothly and without snags. Once you get your own pair of fabric scissors, don't use them on anything else or they will get dull. You'll also need a small pair of craft scissors (near right) to cut the paper patterns.

2. NEEDLES

Embroidery needles have a slightly larger eye that makes them easy to thread, so try using them when sewing.

3. THREAD

Use slightly thicker than normal thread, like the thread made for quilting. It's easier to hold on to while sewing.

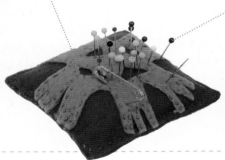

PINCUSHION

Always put your pins and needles into a pincushion when they're not in use. (To make one, see page 21.)

EMBROIDERY THREAD

Use embroidery thread, which is thicker, when you want your stitches to show, or as trim.

SEWING PINS

Sewing pins are used to pin fabric onto the dressmaker dummy, to pin the pattern to the fabric, and to hold fabric together while you sew.

SEAM RIPPER

We all make mistakes. That's when a seam ripper is your best friend. To take out stitches, slide the point of the tiny tool under the stitch and press up.

RULER OR MEASURING TAPE

Use the handy measuring tape included in your kit or a ruler for all projects in the book.

SNAPS & VELCRO

These two fasteners are great for doll-sized clothing because they come in various sizes, including very small.

TAILOR'S CHALK

Special chalk used to mark fabric. It brushes easily away.

SKETCHBOOK

One of the most important fashion design tools. Use a sketchbook to hold your drawings, try out color combos, and tape in inspirations.

TRACING PAPER

Use tracing paper to copy patterns in this kit or to modify patterns to create your own designs.

IRON AND IRONING BOARD

An early lesson in sewing: Everything looks better after it's been pressed with a hot iron. Before using an iron, ask an adult to teach you and read the cautions on page 25.

How the Projects Work

We made this book easy to use so you can create doll-sized fashions with little or no help from an adult. Most projects have a custom-made pattern found at the back of the book. It fits any 11½-inch fashion doll—yes, that means Barbies as well as other dolls of that size.

All the (Mostly) No-Sew Projects in Chapter 5 require little or no sewing. Don't skip these projects even if you know how to sew—they're quick to make and look great as well. The other projects are organized by type of garment—tops and bottoms, skirts, dresses, etc. Each project has a rating of 🖤 (easy), 🖤🖤 (pretty easy), or 🖤🖤🖤 (harder) mannequins at the top. All projects also have a supplies section that are like the ingredients in a cookbook recipe. Gather all these supplies before you start.

We use Sindy dolls as models— aren't they sweet and stylish?

① PREPARING PATTERNS

The paper patterns are printed full-size, so all you have to do is copy (using a photocopier) or trace the pieces of the pattern you'd like to make and cut them out. If tracing, be sure to make note of dotted lines and transfer any other markings (like instructions to pleat, fold, cut, or tie) and labels (like the name and part of the garment, e.g., sleeve, body, etc.) onto the pattern, including the number of pieces you need to cut. Once you've cut out the pattern, pin it to the fabric (see opposite page). When you're finished, put the pattern pieces in the box for another day.

Sometimes the pattern is so simple, we ask you to make your own rectangle by measuring the shape on a piece of paper and cutting it out.

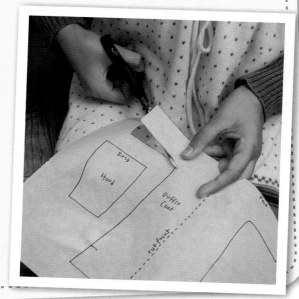

PIN PATTERN TO FABRIC

Lay your fabric flat on a table, either folded or unfolded depending on the pattern instructions, and smooth out any wrinkles.

Look at the pattern pieces carefully and read what they say. Some pieces say to pin along the fold. If the pattern piece doesn't specifically say to align an edge to a fold, then simply lay the pattern piece on the folded fabric, away from any edge, and cut two pieces at once (i.e., a front and a back).

Lay the pattern pieces on top of the fabric so the up-and-down or side-to-side of the finished garment lines up with the side edge (called the selvage), of the fabric. In the case of stretchy materials like cotton jersey, the pattern piece will have an arrow to show which direction the stretch should go.

Using sewing pins, pin the pattern pieces to the fabric by sticking the point through the paper and fabric, and then back out again. Pin once in the center and then pin around the edges of the pattern piece, as shown. Don't let the pins extend off the paper because you'll be cutting around the edges and you don't want the pins to get in the way. If the pattern includes any special marks like dots, darts, or fold lines, draw them onto the fabric with tailor's chalk.

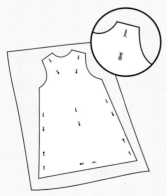

Pin pattern to fabric

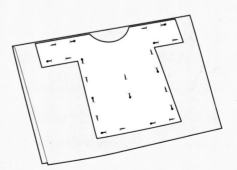

Pin on the fold

CUT FABRIC

Cut carefully around the pattern's edges on the solid line. Stay as close to the paper pattern as you can without cutting into it. Sharp scissors really help here. If there are any marks on the pattern, transfer them to the fabric with tailor's chalk. Now you can remove the pins and put them back into your pincushion.

Tips for cutting

* Slide scissors gently across table so you don't have to lift fabric. You should move rather than the fabric.
* Use this part of the blade when cutting, not the tip.

Telling Right from Wrong

When you fold fabric, sometimes you'll be told to place the "right" or "wrong" sides together. What does this mean? Some fabrics, like cotton prints, jersey, and corduroy, have a front and back that are different in appearance. Usually it's pretty clear which side is meant to be on the outside—this side is called the "right" side. The "wrong" side is the one worn against the skin. When the pattern instruction says, "with right sides together," it means layer or fold the fabric so the right sides, or the top of the fabric, are touching each other. If the pattern instruction says, "with wrong sides together," it means fold the fabric so the wrong sides, or the underneath, of the fabric are touching each other.

Right side (light blue)

Wrong side (dark blue)

PIN FOR SEWING

The project instructions will tell you how to pin the pieces together for sewing. Generally, the pieces are placed one on top of the other with the right sides of the fabric facing each other. Place sewing pins perpendicular to the edge that needs to be sewed in order to keep the garment pieces properly aligned.

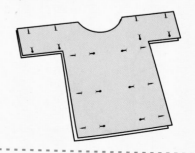

The Dressmaker Dummy

When we say try the garment on the dummy, we don't mean your little brother or sister! Fashion designers use dressmaker dummies all the time to create new designs. They lay or drape muslin fabric on the dummy, then pin, fold, mark, and snip with scissors until it turns into a three-dimensional garment. This piece of muslin is taken off the dummy and becomes the pattern for the real item of clothing.

Your dress form is the same size as your 11½-inch dolls so you can use it to see how your garment fits. Also use the dummy to modify a pattern in this book, create new designs of your own, or model your fashions when they're done. The dress form is made of foam underneath the fabric cover, so you can stick sewing pins through the fabric and into the body to try out your ideas before you cut and sew.

Trying out a new idea on the dress form

A Paper Dress?

Designers use muslin to try out their new designs—it's a beige, inexpensive material readily available in fabric stores. If you don't have any muslin lying around, try using paper towels or brown paper to test out your design. Cut it out, tape up the seams, and try it on the dummy. If you make a mistake adjust your pattern and try again.

To experiment, take a small piece of fabric; fold it, wrap it, and tuck it around the chest until you like how it looks and fits. You've made a shirt. Now take another piece of fabric and wrap it around the waist for a skirt. Pin the waist or tie it with a bit of string. If you want a fuller skirt, try making little folds, or pleats, and pin the fabric as you go around the dummy's body. Keep experimenting with new shapes. Draw a sketch or take a photo of your best outfits before you take them off the dummy.

If you want to alter a pattern in the book, pin the pattern or garment pieces to the dummy and think about what would make it look better—like adding sleeves or changing the length. Maybe you'd like a tighter top or a ruffle at the bottom. Experiment with how this looks on the dummy.

CHAPTER 4

Ready, Set, Sew!

WHY SEW?

You may be asking, why make something when you can buy it just as easily? I like to ask, why buy something when you can make it? Making things is fun, and you wind up with something that is way cooler than anything store-bought could ever be.

* * *

But there's more to it. There's a special pleasure that comes from making something with your own two hands, a piece of cloth, a needle and thread.

Back in the old days, when people had to make things because there were few stores—or because store-bought goods were too expensive—women and girls would come together to craft. Crafting is just a fancy word for making useful stuff and trying to make it pretty or interesting while you're at it. Clothes, quilts, dolls, toys—you name it, people used to make them for themselves and their families. In colonial times,

Isabel sewing a flowered dress for her doll.

friends and family gathered together around a single quilt, making short work of a lot of stitching. It was called a quilting bee.

But in the late 1800s something changed. With the coming of the Industrial Revolution machines could make the same items faster than people, and stores could sell them cheaper than handmade items. So some people began to forget how to make things.

Luckily, the urge to create never really went away. In the twenty-first century, we've seen a full-blown return to sewing, knitting, and do-it-yourself projects.

When we craft, we use our hands, our hearts, our minds and, if we have good crafting buddies, our mouths as we share tips, stories, and jokes.

Besides, sewing is a practical skill that everyone should learn: You never know when you'll need to fix a hem or a ripped seam. And once you do it, you realize it's just plain fun.

People complain that sewing, especially hand sewing, takes a lot of time. Give it a try and you'll see it's faster than you think. Plus, when you include your friends in the activity, you get that extra something that comes with hanging out.

Make a pincushion

Cut two 3-inch squares from a piece of fabric that doesn't unravel, like felt or cotton jersey. Pin the squares together with the wrong sides facing. Sew around the edges with a running stitch (see page 23), about ⅛ inch in from the edge. Stop sewing about 2 inches before you get back to where you started, leaving a small opening. Stuff the cushion with cotton, wool, or polyester stuffing. Sew the opening closed.

If you like, add an appliquéd design (see page 86) to the top of the pincushion before sewing it. Try making a pincushion in a fun shape, like a heart or a star.

Two Basic Stitches

In this section, you'll learn the basics of sewing—how to get started and the only two stitches you'll need to sew anything in this book.

THREADING A NEEDLE

Cut a piece of thread no longer than your arm. Hold the needle in your left hand, the thread in your right hand, and aim the thread for the hole (the "eye") in the needle. Pull the end of 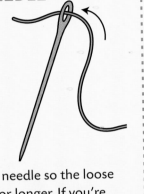 the thread through the needle so the loose end measures 4 inches or longer. If you're having trouble, recut the end and wet it on your tongue. Try again.

MAKING A KNOT

Before you begin to sew, you'll need to make a knot at the long end of the thread. Hold the end of the thread between your thumb and middle finger, and wrap the thread around the tip of your index finger. Slide your thumb forward and middle finger back over the thread until it twists and comes off your finger. Pull the knot toward the end of the thread so it's tight. When sewing, the knot should be on the wrong side, or inside, of your garment.

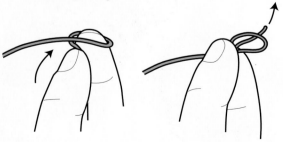

Making a knot

KEEPING THE THREAD ON THE NEEDLE

If you're not careful while you're sewing, your thread may slip out of the eye of the needle. To prevent this, hold on to the needle at the eye so you can hold the needle *and* thread as you work, and keep checking that your loose end is at least 4 inches. Another option is to tie a single knot right around the eye of the needle. This won't interfere with your sewing, but it will keep the thread on the needle.

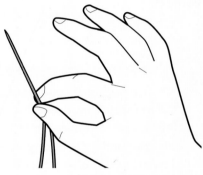

Option 1: Hold the needle at the eye.

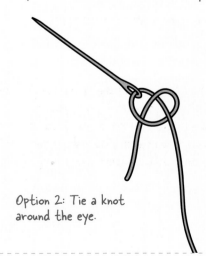

Option 2: Tie a knot around the eye.

STRAIGHT (OR RUNNING) STITCH

You'll use this stitch for all the seams in the projects in this book. To make a straight stitch, bring needle and thread up through the fabric from the underside to the top at point A, and down again from the top to the underside at point B. Pull. Make your stitches small and even with small spaces in between that are the same size as the stitches. With a little practice, you can weave the needle in and out of the fabric until there are several stitches on it, as shown, right. (That's why it's called a "running" stitch.) Then pull the thread all the way through. Good hand sewing has eight stitches to the inch, four on the front and four on the back. But start out aiming for five or six stitches to the inch.

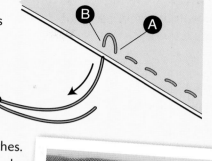

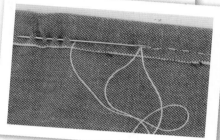

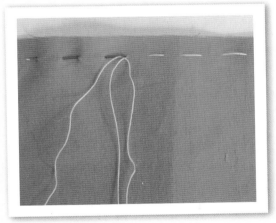

Basting stitch

BASTING STITCH

The basting stitch is a straight stitch using longer stitches. You'll use it to make gathers in the projects. Make each stitch about ¼ inch and use thread that's easy to see and pull out later. Knot only at one end.

KNOT (OR TIE) OFF

Every time you end your stitching (whether it's because you've run out of thread or reached the end of a seam), you'll need to make a knot to secure your stitches. Make one tiny final stitch, but before you pull it tight, bring the needle through the loop created by the stitch. Pull firmly on the thread to make a knot. Cut the thread with scissors to about ½ inch.

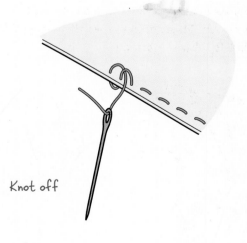

Knot off

BACKSTITCH

Use the backstitch when you want a strong seam or use it every few stitches to make a line of straight stitches stronger. Begin as for a straight stitch by bringing the needle up through the fabric from the back (point A). Then go backward and poke the needle down (point B). Pull the needle up in front of the first stitch (point C) then poke the needle down again at point A. Backstitching makes a solid, unbroken line of stitching, with no spaces, and is great for making shapes or letters in embroidery (see page 62).

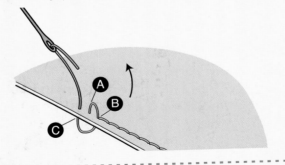

FASTEN

When you want to fasten overlapping fabric, you can sew on Velcro or a snap. Both fasteners have two sides that interlock when pressed together. Separate the two sides and sew to each side of the fabric you want closed.

Velcro

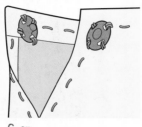

Snap

SEAM ALLOWANCE

The seam allowance is the space between where you make a line of stitching and the edge of your fabric. In our patterns, the seam allowances are ⅛ or ¼ inch, but if you want the clothes a bit smaller or bigger, feel free to change the seam allowance.

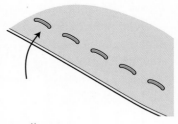

Seam allowance

CLIP ALONG THE CURVE

Curved seams, like necklines and waists, will not lie flat unless you clip the curved edges. As you fold the fabric, make tiny ⅛-inch cuts about ½ inch apart along the curves at the edge of the fabric within the seam allowance. Be careful to keep your cuts small.

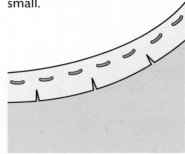

Clipping along the curve allows fabric to lie flat when sewn.

PRESSING SEAMS OPEN

If you have access to an iron (and an adult to teach you how to use it), press each seam open after sewing. Ironing fixes many problems, including messy stitches and uneven seam lines! If you don't have an iron, you can press the seam open with your fingers and your finished garment will look just fine.

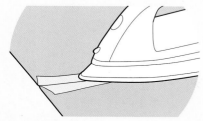

Pressing seams open

HEM

A hem is made to finish the raw edge of a garment, usually the bottom edge. To hem the bottom of your project, turn the fabric under to the inside of the garment, so the wrong sides are together. Pin or press to keep the folded fabric in place and then sew with a running stitch along the raw edge.

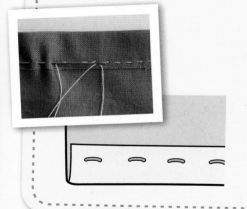

FINISHING EDGES

Sometimes you'll want to turn under and finish the raw fabric edges at the waist, neck, or arms. For example, some projects in the book tell you to stop a seam about 1 inch from the waist. Rather than leaving the edges raw, turn under about ¼ or ⅛ inch and pin or press to hold the fabric in place. Then sew a hem using a running stitch close to the edge.

CHAPTER 5

(Mostly) No-Sew Projects

Fun and Easy Projects to Get You Started

When my kids were little, we had a costume box full to the brim with dozens of pieces of fabric—shimmery, sheer, shiny, and sparkly—all ready to be transformed at a moment's notice into party dresses, royal capes, or even a mermaid's tail. For years, my daughter wrapped, tied, and pinned until she was happy as a clam with the new style she'd created. No need for seams, no sewing; just wrap it, tie it, and go! The easy projects in this chapter require very little sewing. Perfect for beginners and everyone else.

No-Sew Sock Dress and Skirt

Level:

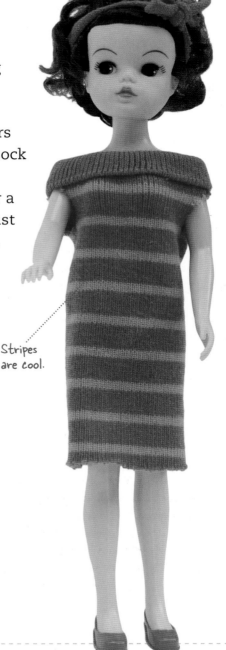

Stripes
are cool.

Nearly everyone who wears shoes has at least one orphan sock lying around. You can use that single sock to make an entire outfit. There's no sewing—just a few snips with the scissors and you're finished! If you don't have a sock you want to sacrifice, any bit of stretchy material—like a piece of an old T-shirt or a rectangle of knitted fabric—will work just as well (see Tube Dress or Skirt, page 30).

Supplies

* **One child-sized sock with a leg that fits over the dressmaker dummy's torso**
* **Scissors**
* **Ruler**

Cut up the sock

Cut the sock apart as shown in the illustration—straight across the toe, across the foot near the heel, and across at the ankle.

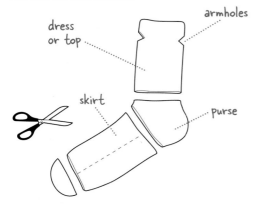

Make the dress

1. Cut two small (approx. ¼-inch) triangles on opposite sides of the sock leg, 1⅛ inches down from the top of the ribbing for armholes, as shown above.

2. Slip the leg of the sock onto the torso of your doll or dummy. Turn down the top 1 inch of the ribbing to cover the armholes you cut. Trim the other end to

the desired length of the dress or top. A long sock makes a dress; a shorter sock makes a top to pair with a skirt.

Make the skirt

1. Wrap the foot of the sock around the body. Tie a belt around the waist made from a piece of ribbon or a strip of sock fabric cut from the toe piece in a thin spiral.

2. Use the sock's heel with its built-in handle as an instant purse.

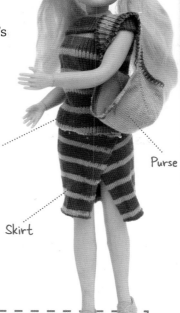

Woven vs. Knit

What's a woven? What's a knit? People get confused all the time about the difference. Knitted fabric, like a T-shirt or a sweater, tends to be more stretchy than woven fabrics. See for yourself by pulling on the edges of a woven cotton like a button-down shirt and some cotton jersey fabric like a T-shirt. The knitted fabric—or the cotton jersey—stretches and the woven fabric—or the cotton print—basically doesn't.

Most woven fabrics will unravel or fray when cut. That's why we hem the raw edges. Cotton jersey doesn't unravel, so you don't need to hem it. Hooray!

Tube Dress or Skirt

Level: 📍

Similar to the sock dress, but without a sock, the tube dress or skirt project does require a little sewing but is about as easy as it gets. Find an old T-shirt you no longer wear in a fun color or stripes and you're ready to get started.

Supplies

* Approximately 6-inch-square piece of cotton jersey, or scrap from an old T-shirt
* Pins
* Newsprint, tracing paper, or wrapping paper for the pattern
* Ruler
* Needle and thread
* Scissors
* Tailor's chalk

Make YOUR OWN Pattern

Belt of cotton jersey

Make the pattern and cut the fabric

1. Make a square paper pattern measuring 5½-inches by 5½-inches.

2. Pin pattern to cotton jersey fabric, lining up a side of the pattern with the ribs (a vertical row of knit stitches—you may have to peer carefully at the fabric to see it) in the fabric.

3. Cut carefully around the pattern edges, and remove pins and pattern.

Make the dress or skirt

1. Tug on the fabric to see which direction stretches more. With the most stretch going left to right, fold the fabric like a book with right sides together. Pin the vertical edges together. This will be the back seam.

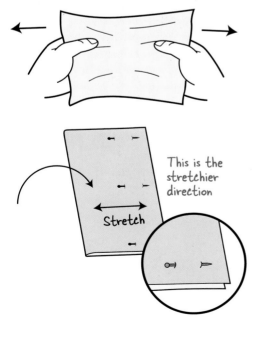

This is the stretchier direction

Stretch

2. With a straight stitch, sew along the back seam, ¼ inch in from the edge for a tube dress or ½ inch in from the edge for a tube skirt. Remove any pins.

Finishing the dress

1. If you're making a dress, find the center front, which is opposite the back seam. At the center top, start ⅛ inch down and sew a ½-inch-long stitch. Pull stitch tightly to gather dress at the bustline and make a knot on the inside.

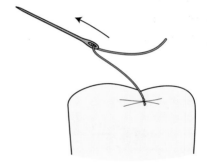

2. Use a strip of cotton jersey or a ribbon, about ½-inch by 6-inches, as a belt and tie at the waist.

VARIATION
Knit-a-Dress

Do you knit? If you do, it's easy to make a nifty knitted dress. Knit a rectangle approximately 5½-inches by 5½-inches and follow the instructions for the tube dress or skirt. Almost any stitch works, but knitting in a rib stitch—that's alternating knits and purls (for example, K1, P1 or K2, P2) across each row—helps the dress fit better.

Martha's No-Sew Circle Dress

Level: 🖉

This dress is more like a trick than a sewing project. A few careful folds and cuts, and you have an adorable dress. We were waiting in line at the annual Claryville, New York, pig roast, when my friend Martha grabbed a paper napkin and showed me how to make this fabulously simple dress. She used to make these dresses by the dozen when she was a kid.

Use a piece of trim for a headband.

Supplies

* **12-inch by 12-inch piece of lightweight woven cotton fabric**
* **Tailor's chalk**
* **Scissors**
* **Needle and thread**
* **Two 5-inch pieces of very thin ribbon (or two 6-inch pieces of embroidery thread) for the ties**
* **6-inch piece of ribbon for belt (optional)**

PATTERN included

Try this wraparound version, step 3, right.

Cut the fabric

1. Copy or trace the pattern (page 118) and cut along the solid lines.

2. Fold fabric in half, with wrong sides together. Line the straight edge of the pattern along the fold. Pin the pattern through both layers.

3. Cut carefully around the neck, the pattern's curved edges, and on the lines marked "cut for armhole." Mark dots on fabric with tailor's chalk. Remove pins and pattern.

Make the dress

1. Before unfolding the fabric, sew one end of each ribbon at the dots you marked on the fold. If you're using embroidery thread, sew one stitch at the fold. Knot off.

2. Try the dress on doll or dummy, tie ribbons or threads into a bow in the back. The extra fabric will fold around the back along the dashes (or fold lines) underneath the armhole.

3. Instead of following step 2, cut a straight line up the center front of the dress, wrap the dress around the doll and tie with a ribbon.

Printed vs. Woven Patterns

If you look carefully, you'll be able to tell whether the patterns on your fabric are printed or woven. Fabrics with designs are usually printed on top of already woven fabric. Since it's printed only on one side, the design is less sharp on the back, or wrong, side of the printed fabric. Plaids or stripes are most often woven into the fabric, so the design appears the same on both sides. This info will come in handy when cutting out a pattern and sewing.

Right side

Wrong side

Printed Pattern

Same on both sides

Woven Pattern

Sarong Dress

Level:

Throughout Africa, Southeast Asia, India, and the Pacific Islands, men and women alike wear beautifully decorated lengths of fabric, called pareos, saris, togas, or sarongs in different cultures. By wrapping and tying they turn them into skirts and dresses. Once you've given this project a try, experiment and see what other ways you can invent to wrap and tie.

A thin piece of leather makes a great belt.

Embroider stripes on your sarong (see page 62).

Supplies

* **Approximately 15-inch by 9-inch piece of lightweight woven cotton fabric**
* **Newsprint, tracing paper, or wrapping paper for the pattern**
* **Ruler**
* **Needle and thread**
* **Scissors**
* **10-inch piece of yarn or string for a belt (or make a belt, see page 92)**
* **Tailor's chalk**
* **Velcro**

Make YOUR OWN Pattern

Make the pattern and cut the fabric

1. To make the paper pattern, measure and draw a rectangle 14-inches by 8-inches. Cut it out.

2. Pin pattern to fabric. Cut carefully around the pattern edges. Remove pins and pattern.

Make the sarong

1. Lay the fabric on a table with the wrong side facing up. Fold the edges of the rectangle ¼ inch toward the wrong side, pinning or pressing with an iron as you go.

2. Sew folded edges down ⅛ inch in from the edge.

Note: You can skip this step if you don't feel like hemming, or don't mind if the fabric unravels a bit.

Wrap the dress

1. Wrap the fabric around the dummy following these steps: First, line up the center of the long side of the fabric with the center back and under arms of the dressmaker dummy (or doll).

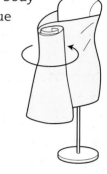

2. Second, grab the top corners with one hand and hold away from the body of the dummy.

3. Fold or roll the fabric, beginning at the top corners and making small folds toward the body of the dummy. Continue folding until it's pretty tight at the chest and waist.

4. Tie with a piece of fabric or a belt at the waist.

VARIATION
Wrap Skirt

1. Start with a paper pattern measuring 7½-inches by 4-inches and hem around the edges as in "Make the Sarong," above.

2. If you'd like to tie the wrap skirt, sew a 6-inch piece of ribbon to each top corner of the skirt.

3. Wrap the skirt one and one half times around the dummy, overlapping, as shown, and tie the ribbons on the side or back. Or wrap and mark with chalk where to attach the Velcro to keep the skirt closed, then sew on.

Tops & Bottoms

T-shirts and tank tops are not only popular but very versatile—they come in so many different shapes and colors that you'll never get tired of them. Plus, they're easy to make, so our tops in this chapter are variations on the Tee. Think about recycling an old T-shirt for these projects—but ask your Mom or Dad before you start cutting.

Ask any girl and she'll tell you: Skirts are fun, but pants are where it's at if you want to run, play, and stay warm. Before movie stars Katharine Hepburn and Greta Garbo began wearing pants in the 1940s, women in America simply didn't. Pants were a practical choice during World War II when women worked in factories, and once they saw how comfortable pants were, they never looked back.

PROJECTS

Simple Tank

Level: ![dress form icon]

Did you know that people in the early twentieth century used to call swimming pools swimming tanks? And tank tops got their name because they resembled the tops of old-fashioned swimsuits. Not long ago, the tank top would have only been worn underneath your clothes or at the gym. Nowadays, you are as likely to see a tank on a jogger as you are to see one paired with a party skirt and decorated with appliqués, sequins, or beads. A longer tank makes a great dress, so we've included a pattern for that, too.

Supplies

* **13-inch-square piece of cotton jersey fabric, old T-shirt, or any other stretchy fabric (this is enough fabric to make both a tank shirt and tank dress)**
* **Ruler**
* **Needle and thread**
* **Scissors**

PATTERN
included

For Two-in-One
Trousers project,
see page 46

Note: Cotton jersey stretches more in one direction than the other—with T-shirts the most stretch goes across the body. So be careful to follow the instructions about how to fold the fabric so that clothes will stretch in the right direction.

Cut the fabric

1. Copy or trace pattern for the tank top. Cut out paper pattern.

2. Tug on the fabric to see which direction stretches more. With the stretch going left to right, fold the fabric with right sides together so the stretch runs in the same direction as (or is parallel to) the fold.

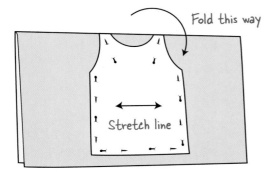

Fold this way

Stretch line

3. Pin the pattern to the fabric through both layers of fabric along the fold at the shoulders of the tank top, as shown.

4. Cut carefully around the pattern edges, and remove pins and pattern.

Make the top

With right sides of fabric together, pin along the side seams and with the straight stitch sew ⅛ inch in from the edge. For a more fitted tank top, use a ¼-inch seam allowance. Turn tank right side out.

No need to hem because cotton jersey doesn't unravel.

Make a Dress

For a tank dress, use the Simple Tank Dress pattern on page 123 and follow the instructions for the Simple Tank, above.

E-Z T-Shirt

Level: ♟

In the 1950s, film stars Marlon Brando and James Dean shocked the moviegoing public by appearing on screen in their white T-shirts. Shock led to fascination and the love affair with the T-shirt has been going strong ever since. Like the tank top project, the E-Z T-Shirt pattern is pinned on the fold so the fold becomes the shoulders. You can choose long or short sleeves.

Supplies

* **Cotton jersey fabric, old T-shirt, or any stretchy fabric (a 12-inch square is enough fabric to make either the T-shirt or T-shirt dress)**
* **Ruler**
* **Needle and thread**
* **Scissors**

PATTERN included

Drawstring Picnic Skirt, page 54

Cut the fabric

1. Choose long or short sleeves and copy or trace the pattern on page 120, and cut out. If you want short sleeves, cut on the line indicated.

2. Tug on the fabric to see which direction stretches more. With the stretch going left to right, fold the fabric, with right sides together, so the stretch runs in the same direction as (or parallel to) the fold.

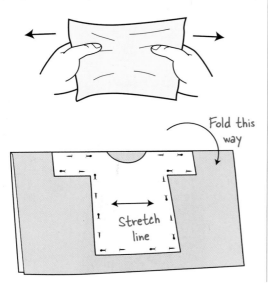

Fold this way

Stretch line

3. Pin the pattern to the fabric along the fold through both layers. The fold will be the shoulder of the T-shirt.

4. Cut carefully around the pattern edges, and remove pins and pattern.

Make the T-shirt

With the right sides of the fabric together, pin sides and sleeves. Using a straight stitch, sew side and sleeve seams ⅛ inch in from the edge. For a tighter fitting T, leave a ¼-inch seam allowance. Turn the T-shirt right side out.

Make a Dress

Use the E-Z T-Dress pattern on page 121 and follow the instructions for the E-Z T-Shirt project, above.

T For Me, T For You

The T-shirt is a walking billboard. Anyone with anything to say, sell, or promote, prints their message or logo on a T-shirt. The oldest printed T-shirt in the Smithsonian Museum says, "Dew-it With Dewey," from Thomas Dewey's 1948 presidential campaign. Mickey Mouse T-shirts weren't far behind. These days, rock bands print their album cover art on them. Punk rockers ripped them and then safety-pinned them back together again. Make your T-shirt your own.

Challenge T or T-Dress

Level: ♦♦♦

Shoulder seams make this look like a real T-shirt.

Try the Challenge T after you've mastered the E-Z T-Shirt and are ready for something new. In this project, the body and arms of the T-shirt or T-dress are not all in one piece, so you'll learn the very useful skill of insetting sleeves, which will come in handy later on when you start designing your own full-sized fashions.

Supplies

* **Cotton jersey fabric, old T-shirt, or any stretchy fabric (a 12-inch square is enough fabric to make either the T-Shirt or T-Dress)**
* **Ruler**
* **Needle and thread**
* **Scissors**

PATTERN included

For Two-in-One Trousers, see page 46

Make It

Cut the fabric

1. Choose the T-shirt or dress and copy or trace the two pattern pieces: body and sleeve on pages 120–121. Notice that you can choose short or long sleeves. Cut out pattern pieces.

2. Tug on the fabric to see which direction stretches more. With the stretch going left to right, fold the fabric in half, so the stretch runs in the same direction as (or parallel to) the fold. See page 41.

3. Pin patterns to the fabric through both layers, making sure the stretch direction of the fabric matches the stretch line on the pattern.

4. Cut carefully around the pattern edges, and remove pins and patterns. You will have four pieces: a T-shirt or dress front, T-shirt or dress back, and two sleeves.

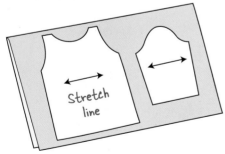

Stretch line

Make the T-shirt or dress

1. Lay the body pieces on top of each other with the right sides of fabric together. Pin the shoulder seams together and sew across both shoulders ⅛ inch in from the edge.

Nothing is more comfortable than a T-dress.

2. Open up the body of the T-shirt or dress and place it on a table with the right side facing up. With the right sides together, pin the curved part of the sleeves to the shoulder seams; begin by matching up and pinning the center, left, and right edges of the sleeve with the body armhole. You may need to ease, or stretch, the fabric a bit to fit the sleeve into the armhole.

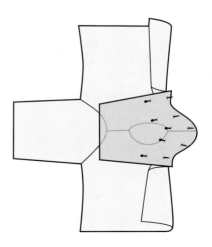

3. Sew with a ⅛-inch seam allowance along the pinned edge. Repeat with second sleeve.

4. With right sides together, pin the side and sleeve seams and sew ⅛ inch in from the edge. Turn finished T-shirt right side out.

VARIATIONS ON THE T-SHIRT

Hoodie Power

For a cute hoodie, begin by making a long sleeve T (either the E-Z T or the Challenge T).

1. Copy or trace the pattern for a hood (see Little Red Cape hood pattern, page 118).

2. Fold a small piece of cotton jersey, with fabric right sides together (don't worry about the direction of the stretch). Pin the pattern through both layers of fabric along the fold as marked, and cut.

3. Pin right sides of the hood together and sew the back seam.

This hoodie has a pocket.

4. With right sides of the hood and T-shirt together, and beginning at the center of the back, pin the hood to the T-shirt along the neckline. Sew along the neckline.

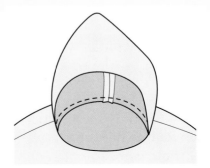

Cardigan

Cut down the front of the long-sleeved T-shirt and you have a cardigan. Leave open, sew on tiny buttons, or close with tiny pieces of Velcro or snaps.

Twinsets—a matching pullover and cardigan—were popular, worn with pearls, in the 1950s.

Print Your Own Fabric

Think of your fabric as a blank piece of paper. With fabric paint or markers, you can draw, paint, or print your own designs and you'll wind up with a one-of-a-kind piece of fabric. Find some light-colored cotton fabric—either woven or jersey—and try out some of our ideas below:

1. Draw with markers.
2. Paint with fabric paint.
3. Buy a stencil at the craft store, or cut your own from a piece of heavyweight card stock. Use stencils and fabric paint to create designs.
4. Decorate with rubber stamps. Dip the stamps in fabric paint.
5. Potato prints. Cut a small potato in half, carve a design with a knife into the flat side, dip in fabric paint, and press carefully onto the fabric.
6. Iron-on transfers. Your local stationery or craft store will likely carry iron-on paper that will work with your computer printer.
7. Dye or tie-dye your fabric with Rit® dye from the supermarket.
8. Print your own fabric from a computer. Stationery and craft stores also sell fabric that fits into your computer printer so you can create a design on your computer and print it directly onto the fabric. You can even print photos on the fabric.
9. For your favorite designs, you can order custom-printed fabric by the yard, available online from print-on-demand companies like Spoonflower (www .spoonflower.com).

You can make all kinds of shapes with potato prints.

Two-in-One Trousers

Level:

A skinny strip of fabric makes a fun scarf.

If you've ever gone into a dressing room with a pile of blue jeans to try on, you'll know that slight differences in shape can make a big difference in the way they fit. Pants patterns all have one thing in common—a curve for the crotch. The curve is what makes the two-dimensional piece of fabric fit around your three-dimensional body. And once you know how to make pants, you can adjust them to fit perfectly!

Plaids are woven with different color threads.

Supplies

* 8-inch-square piece of cotton, denim, corduroy, wool (for regular trousers/blue jeans) or of cotton jersey fabric, or a piece of an old T-shirt (for leggings)
* Ruler
* Scissors
* Needle and thread
* Velcro or a snap (for regular pants only)

PATTERN included

Make It

Note: This is a two-in-one pattern. Cut on one line for close-fitting leggings, and on the other for a regular fit trouser. Make sure to use stretchy fabric (like cotton jersey) for the leggings or they won't fit.

Cut the fabric

1. Copy or trace the Two-in-One Trousers pattern on page 125. Decide between leggings and regular pants and cut out the paper pattern along the appropriate line.

2. Fold fabric in half and pin pattern to fabric on the fold. For the leggings, tug on the fabric to see which direction stretches more (see page 41). With the stretch going left to right, fold the fabric in half like a book with the stretch running against, or perpendicular to, the fold.

3. Cut carefully around the pattern edges, and remove pins and pattern.

4. Repeat steps 2 and 3 so you have two identical pieces. This is confusing at first, but you'll soon see that each fabric piece makes one of the legs. Unfold the fabric.

Make the pants or leggings

1. With right sides together, lay the two pieces of pants fabric on top of each other.

2. Pin the front and back crotches together. Sew ⅛ inch in from the edges along the curved edge between the crotch and the waist. For the blue jeans/trousers, leave the back crotch seam open 1¼ inches at the top or waist edge, as shown.

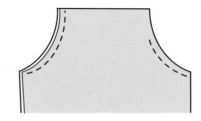

3. With right sides still together, open and reposition the pants or leggings pieces so that the crotch seams are one on top of each other. Now you can see the two separate legs! Pin together the raw edges of each leg separately.

4. Sew ⅛ inch in from the edges, starting at the bottom of one leg, going up the inside of one leg and down the other. Remove any pins.

5. For the pants, fold the raw edges of the back crotch seam under ⅛ inch toward the wrong side and sew. (See Finishing Edges page 25.)

Finish the pants or leggings

1. At the waist, turn down ½ inch toward the wrong side of the fabric and pin in place.

2. Straight stitch around the waist about ¼ inch in from the fold. Turn pants or leggings right side out.

3. For the pants, the back seams should overlap a bit at the top. Try pants on a doll and mark where closure should go. Sew on a snap or Velcro at the waist to close them.

Make leggings (above) or shorts (right).

4. If you want a bottom hem, turn pants inside out. Turn under a ½ inch on the bottom of each leg and sew.

VARIATION

Who wears short shorts?

To make long shorts or shorter shorts, crop the Two-in-One Trousers pattern.

True Blue

You could say that blue jeans are the most important American invention, and you'd be right in my book.

When I was a kid, blue jeans were called "Levi's" after Levi Strauss, the man who invented them. Strauss, a 24-year-old German Jewish immigrant headed to San Francisco in 1853 when he heard about the California Gold Rush. There he set up a wholesale dry-goods business selling the cotton twill fabric known as denim. Gold miners complained that their trousers weren't strong enough for their rough job, so Strauss teamed up with tailor Jacob Davis to make work pants out of the sturdy denim fabric with rivets to reinforce the stress points. The two patented this idea in 1873 and blue jeans were born.

"Jeans have expression, modesty, sex appeal, and simplicity—I wish I had invented them," said the famous French designer Yves Saint Laurent.

Cozy Lounge Pants

Level: 🎎

These are the kind of pants that you want to wear when you snuggle up on the couch in front of the fireplace. They're comfy, cozy, and completely essential.

See Challenge T project on page 42.

Flannel fabric is cozy!

Supplies

* 6-inch by 8-inch piece of flannel, cotton, T-shirt, sweatshirt, or velour fabric
* Scissors
* Ruler
* Needle and thread
* 15-inch-long piece of string or very thin (⅛-inch) ribbon or twill tape (for drawstring)

PATTERN included

Cut the fabric

1. Copy or trace the pattern on page 128. Cut out paper pattern.

2. Fold fabric with right sides together and pin pattern to fabric along the fold. Cut carefully around the pattern edges, and remove pins and pattern. Repeat so you have two identical pieces, one for each leg. Unfold the fabric.

Make the pants

1. With right sides together, place the two pieces directly on top of each other.

2. Pin the front crotch and back crotch seams as marked on the pattern piece.

3. On one side, you'll need to leave an opening for the drawstring. Starting at the waist, sew only about ½ inch of the front crotch seam, leaving a ⅛-inch seam allowance.  Knot off and cut thread. Begin sewing again ¼ inch down the seam, which leaves a ¼-inch opening for the drawstring (see illustration).

4. Sew the back crotch seam ⅛ inch in from the edge.

5. With right sides still together, open and reposition the pants so that the

crotch seams are on top of each other. Now you can see two separate legs! Pin together the raw edges of each leg separately.

6. Make the leg seams by sewing ⅛ inch in from the edges, starting at the bottom of one leg, going up the inside of that leg and down the other. Remove any pins.

Finish the pants

1. At the waist, make the drawstring casing by turning down ½ inch toward wrong side of fabric, and pin in place.

2. Place the drawstring under the waistband fold and thread the ends through the opening in the front crotch seam.

3. Sew along the raw edge of the casing, being careful not to catch the drawstring.

4. Turn pants right side out and try on doll. Pull drawstring and tie ends in a bow. Roll up the pants legs for a casual look.

CHAPTER 7

Skirts

The Long and Short of It

The history of the skirt is a long and short story. The skirt is the second oldest garment known to mankind (the first is the loincloth). Hemlines have gone up and down, and up again. Skirts have been full with lots of layers, or fitted with barely room for even a pair of tights underneath. Nowadays, skirts come in many shapes; they can be full, bouncy, slinky, slim, bell-shaped, A-line, or tiered.

Mod Mini 1-2-3 Skirt

Level: ♟

The 1960s were a time of liberation and nothing was more liberating than a miniskirt! Several designers have claimed to be the inventor of the mini, but it was English designer Mary Quant who made the miniskirt popular. She also coined the name—after her favorite English car, the Mini. She paired her mini with colored tights to make an outfit that looks great but is comfortable enough to wear running for the bus.

Supplies

* A 5½-inch by 11-inch piece of fabric will make the straight or the A-line skirt. Almost any kind of fabric will work: woven cotton, wool, denim, silk.
* Ruler
* Small piece of Velcro or a snap
* Tailor's chalk
* Needle and thread
* Scissors
* Iron (optional)

PATTERN included

① Mini-straight skirt

See Knee Socks on page 89

Note: This pattern is a two-in-one pattern. Follow one set of lines on the pattern and make a straight skirt. Follow the other set of lines and make a classic A-line skirt (a name invented by designer Christian Dior to describe his flared skirt). Next choose the mini or the knee length. It's all up to you.

A-line skirt

Straight, knee-length skirt

Cut the fabric

1. Choose the skirt you'd like to make—straight or A-line, mini or to the knee. Copy or trace the pattern on page 119. Cut out paper pattern.

2. Fold the fabric in half with right sides together. Pin the pattern to the fabric on the fold as indicated.

3. Cut carefully around the pattern edges. Remove pins and pattern.

Make the skirt

1. Since the waist is curved, it will not lie flat unless you make about six tiny ⅛-inch cuts along the curved edge with your scissors. (See Clip Along the Curve, page 24.) Pin or press in place.

Along the top of the skirt, fold over ¼ inch toward the wrong side of fabric.

2. Stitch along the folded top of the skirt ⅛ inch in from the edge.

3. With right sides together, fold the skirt in half and pin the back seam. Beginning at the bottom of the skirt, sew the back seam ⅛ inch in from the edge, stopping the stitching 1 inch from the top.

4. At the top of the back seam, turn under the two raw edges ⅛ inch and stitch. (See Finishing Edges, page 25.)

5. At the bottom of the skirt, turn under ½ inch toward the wrong side and sew ¼ inch from the folded edge to make a hem. Turn skirt right side out.

6. Try the skirt on the dummy or doll to check the fit at the waist. With chalk or a pin, mark placement for a Velcro or a small snap closure at the waist. Remove the skirt, and sew in place. (See Fasten, page 24.)

Drawstring Picnic Skirt

Level: ♟♟

This skirt makes me think of sitting on a picnic blanket with Alice (yes, in Wonderland) on a beautiful sunny day on the banks of a winding English river, with the pretty fabric of my full-flowered skirt fanning out around me. My favorite versions of this skirt were made of beautiful Liberty floral cottons from England— just like Alice!

Liberty floral prints are my favorite!

Supplies

* **Less than a ½ yard of cotton or silk fabric—one that makes you happy**
* **Newsprint, tracing, or wrapping paper for the pattern**
* **Ruler**
* **Scissors**
* **Needle and thread**
* **24-inch-long piece of string, yarn, or ⅛-inch-wide ribbon**
* **Small safety pin**
* **Tailor's chalk**

Make YOUR OWN Pattern

Make the pattern and cut the fabric

1. Measure and draw a rectangle 18-inches by 5-inches on paper (or 15-inches by 5-inches for a less full skirt). Cut out.

2. Pin pattern to fabric ½ inch in from the selvage edge or, if you're using a scrap, wherever it will fit. Cut carefully around the pattern edges, and remove pins and pattern.

Make the drawstring casing

1. With wrong side facing up, place the fabric on a table. Along one long side, fold down ¾ inch toward the wrong side of fabric. Pin or press with your iron.

2. Straight stitch a line, about ½ inch from the fold, all the way across. Remove any pins. This creates the drawstring casing, the place where the drawstring will go.

Make the skirt

1. With the drawstring casing at the top, fold the fabric in half like a book with right sides together, so it measures 9-inches by 4¼-inches. Pin the edges together along the short sides.

2. Beginning just below the drawstring casing, straight stitch along the pinned edge to make the back seam. Be sure to leave the ends

of the drawstring casing open so you can insert the drawstring later. Remove the pins. You will have a tube.

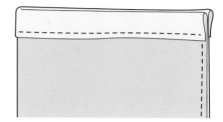

3. To make hem, fold the bottom edge of the skirt up ½ inch toward the wrong side of the fabric and sew around the folded edge. Turn the skirt right side out.

Thread the drawstring and finish the skirt

1. Make a small knot at the end of the yarn or ribbon you're using as a drawstring. Pin the safety pin to the knot.

2. Push the safety pin (and the drawstring along with it) into the casing opening. Through the fabric, grab the safety pin and use it to push and pull the drawstring through the

casing until it comes out the other side. Remove the safety pin.

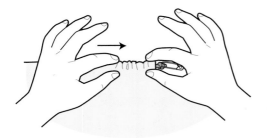

3. Try your new skirt on the dressmaker dummy (or a doll), pull the drawstring tight around the waist, and tie in a bow at the back.

VARIATION
Poufy Netting Skirt
Think ballerina tutu and you'll come close to this fun variation. Layers and layers of tulle or netting are poufy, sassy, and party-ready.

1. Make a 15-inch by 4-inch paper pattern. Netting is hard to keep in place when cutting, so start by cutting out about nine pieces of netting, each larger than the pattern piece. Nine pieces of netting make a great, really poufy skirt.

2. On a table, stack the pieces of netting into a neat pile, pin the pattern to the layers of fabric, and cut around the pattern through all the layers. Pull on the top edge of the

bottom layer and fold it down ¾ inch over the long edge of the rest of the layers. Pin through all nine layers. Sew ½ inch down from the fold to secure all the layers together. This forms the drawstring casing. With scissors, trim the bottom edges of the skirt so all layers are even.

3. Sew the back seam and thread the drawstring through the casing, as above.

4. Let's dance!

Swirly Skirt

Level: ♟♟♟

Little House on the Prairie meets hippie chic! Call it what you like—prairie skirt, gypsy skirt—the Swirly Skirt is a style that never seems to get old. This may be because it looks so good on women or girls of many different sizes and shapes, or maybe because it's so comfortable. The basic concept is simple: Each of the tiers is two times wider than the one above it. This creates a skirt that will swish and sway when you walk, and swirl when you dance.

See E-Z T-Shirt on page 40

Supplies:

* **About ¼ yard of lightweight cotton fabric**
* **Newsprint, tracing paper, or wrapping paper for the pattern**
* **Scissors**
* **Ruler**
* **Tailor's chalk**
* **Needle and thread**
* **Iron (optional)**

PATTERN included

Make the pattern and cut the fabric

1. Copy or trace the pattern on page 127 for Tier 1. Cut out paper pattern. For Tiers 2 and 3, make paper patterns for two rectangles: one that's 12-inches by 2-inches and another that's 24-inches by 2-inches. Label the smaller pattern Tier 2 and the larger one Tier 3.

2. Fold a small piece of fabric, and pin the pattern for Tier 1 on the fold as marked on the pattern. Cut carefully around the pattern edges, and remove pins and pattern. Unfold and put Tier 1 aside.

3. Pin the pattern pieces for Tiers 2 and 3 onto the fabric. Note that for pattern pieces two and three there's no need to fold the fabric. Cut carefully around the edges of the patterns, and remove pins and patterns.

Make the skirt: Tier 1

1. Along the top of Tier 1 fold down edge ¼ inch toward the wrong side of fabric. This will be the waist. To make the waist lie flat, make about six tiny ⅛-inch cuts where marked along the curved edge of the fabric using your scissors (see Clip Along the Curve, page 24), and pin or press in place.

2. Sew along the folded edge about ⅛ inch in from the edge.

3. Using a ruler and chalk, measure and mark along the raw bottom edge to divide the fabric into quarters, marking the ¼, ½, and ¾ points. You will need these markings later. Set aside Tier 1.

Make Tiers 2 and 3

1. Sew long basting stitches (see page 23) along one long side of Tier 2. This will be the top of Tier 2. Using tailor's chalk, mark the ¼, ½, and ¾ points along the top of Tier 2 as you did for Tier 1 above.

2. Repeat for Tier 3.

3. With right sides together, match the right and left edges and the ¼,

½, and ¾ chalk markings on the top of Tier 2 to the bottom of Tier 1, and pin at each spot. Pull both ends of the basting thread on Tier 2 so the fabric gathers until it is the same width as Tier 1.

4. With your fingers, spread the gathers evenly, then pin and sew Tier 2 to Tier 1 at ¼ inch in from the raw edges.

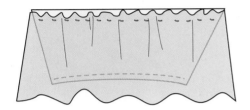

5. Repeat to attach the top of Tier 3 to the bottom of Tier 2. Remove pins and all basting stitches.

Finish the skirt

1. To help the skirt lie flat, from the inside of the skirt, use an iron (or your fingers) to press the seam allowance up toward the waist of the skirt and stitch in place close to the seam through all layers of fabric (see photo, right).

2. Fold skirt in half, with right sides together. Starting at the bottom, sew the back seam, stopping 1 inch from the top. Turn each raw edge of the back seam under ¼ inch and straight stitch close to the fold. (See page 23.)

3. Turn the bottom of skirt under ¼ inch toward the wrong side and sew ⅛ inch in from the folded edge to make a hem. Or, if you like, leave the bottom edge raw. Turn the skirt right side out.

4. Try skirt on dummy or doll. At the waist, use chalk or a pin to mark the placement of Velcro or a small snap. Remove skirt, and sew on the closure. (See Fasten, page 24.)

right side

wrong side

Classic Kilt

Level:

Tank top, page 38

The kilt is a classic, always in style. Originally worn by Scottish men in battle, kilts were later adopted by schoolgirls the world over. For this project you will definitely need an iron to press the pleats, and maybe—since irons are very hot—even a bit of help from an adult. Otherwise, this is an easy project, basically a pleated wraparound skirt. Full-sized kilts come with kilt pins to keep them from flying open, but for this tiny kilt, a small safety pin will work just fine.

Fringed edges

Supplies:

* **Less than ½ yard of wool or flannel plaid fabric**
* **Scissors**
* **Ruler**
* **Needle and thread**
* **Tailor's chalk**
* **Iron**
* **Velcro or snap**
* **Small safety pin**

PATTERN included

Clutch Handbag, page 95

Cut the fabric

1. Copy or trace kilt pattern on page 124. If tracing, be sure to mark the fold lines for the pleats. Cut out paper pattern.

2. Pin pattern to the plaid fabric being careful to line up the straight edges of the pattern with the plaid's lines. Cut carefully around the pattern edges, and remove pins and pattern. Keep pattern handy for pleats.

3. Fringe the two short edges by pulling out a few of the threads so there is about ⅛ inch of fringe.

Make the skirt

1. Fold top of kilt down ¼ inch toward the wrong side of fabric, as marked on the pattern piece, pin or press, and stitch along the raw edge.

2. Turn under ½ inch at bottom edge toward the wrong side of the fabric, and stitch along the raw edge to make a hem.

Iron and sew the pleats

1. Make the five pleats. Place the paper pattern on top of skirt fabric, and using a ruler and tailor's chalk, mark dotted lines for each pleat fold line on the kilt. Working from left to right, make a fold along each dotted line, one at a time. Press each fold with a hot iron until the crease holds its shape. Continue folding and pressing until you've folded all five pleats.

2. Beginning at the top edge of each pleat, sew a line of straight stitching 1¼ inches down each pleat. These stitches will show, so stitch carefully and sew close to the folded edge.

3. Wrap the kilt around a doll or the dummy. At the top where the front fringed edge overlaps, mark with chalk or a pin to show where to sew on a piece of Velcro or a small snap closure. Remove skirt, and sew Velcro or snap in place. Attach a small safety pin near the bottom to act as a kilt pin.

Embroidery

Embroidery is the name for decorating fabric with colorful stitching. I'll tell you a little secret . . . embroidery is much easier than it looks. It may look complicated, but really, it's like drawing with a needle and thread. And you can embroider something really special-looking with just the simple straight stitch you know.

We've included embroidery thread in your kit. It comes in hundreds of different colors. Most embroidery thread is made up of six smaller strands. It is easy to separate the strands and stitch with just one or two strands for a thin line, or use all six for a thicker one.

If you're having trouble threading your needle, fold the thread over the needle and press the fold between your thumb and forefinger so just a bit of the folded edge sticks out. Then push the fold through the eye of the needle.

STITCHES

Straight Stitch
(see page 23)
Since your stitching is for show, stitch carefully. This means your stitches should be even—all the same length and with the same amount of space between each stitch.

Fill Stitch
If you want to fill a space with color, make many straight stitches close to each other to fill in the shape. Make your stitches small—about ¼ inch or smaller works best—so they won't get caught on something and get pulled out.

Embroidered flowers are easy when you know how (see next page).

Backstitch

If you want to make a continuous line with no breaks in it, use the backstitch (see page 24).

Leaves and Flowers

Try this simple embroidery trick: Sew up through the fabric where you want a leaf or petal (A) and down right next to it (B). Pull the thread but leave a small loop. Flatten the loop—or leaf—down on the fabric and from underneath make a tiny stitch to hold the petal/leaf in place.

Stitch holds leaf in place.

SUPPLIES

* *Needle and embroidery thread*
* *Embroidery hoop (unless your fabric is stiff like canvas or wool)*
* *Scissors*
* *Tailor's chalk*

1. Plan your design. Draw a sketch or copy something from a book.

2. Transfer your design to the fabric. You can sketch directly on the fabric with chalk or a pencil or, if you prefer, cut out the shape from your sketchbook and trace the outline onto the fabric, or use dressmaker's carbon paper.

3. Put your fabric in the embroidery hoop. The hoop keeps the fabric flat and taut, which makes it easier to sew your designs.

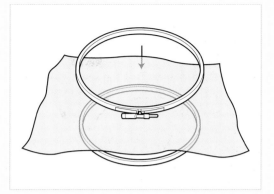

4. Using embroidery thread, stitch along the lines of your design using the straight stitch or backstitch. Change colors as you like.

You can embroider anything you can draw—a tiny house with a flower garden in front, a big bear, a dog, a car, some flowers, circles, letters, butterflies, beetles, boats, bicycles, and . . . I could go on and on. I'll change what I said before; anything you can THINK of, you can draw and embroider. Be careful, though. Embroidery is addictive—once you start, it's hard to stop!

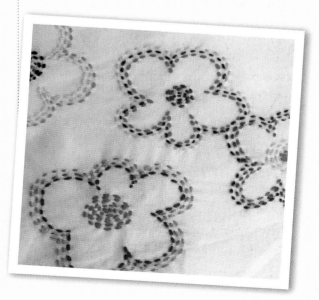

CHAPTER 8

Dresses

Go Girly!

Even though girls and women these days are wearing pants as much as they are dresses, the international symbol for *our* restroom is still a stick figure wearing a dress. Dresses are the most perfectly feminine garments there are, and they're also easy. Pull one on and you're . . . well, dressed. Wear a fancy one, and you're dressed up.

Summer Shift Dress

Level: 🔵

Y ou've heard of paper dolls, but did you know that in the 1960s people wore paper dresses? In 1966 the Scott Paper Company did a marketing promotion—send in one dollar, and you got a full-sized paper dress. It was a huge success and many companies followed suit with paper garments. The frenzy led *Time* magazine to write: "Paper clothing, apparently, is here to stay." It's too bad that prediction was wrong! A paper dress sounds kind of great—hem it with scissors, mend it with tape, and no washing!

Supplies

* **7-inch by 10-inch piece of fabric: wool, cotton, canvas, heavy silk, even paper, or heavy plastic**
* **Scissors**
* **Ruler**
* **Needle and thread**

PATTERN included

I love large-scale prints.

Note: This dress has raw, unfinished edges at the neck and armholes, so it's easy to make, and a great project for beginners. Choose a fabric that won't unravel too much. For a more finished look—and a bit more sewing—try the Challenge Shift Dress on the next page.

Cut the fabric

1. Copy or trace pattern on page 122, and cut out paper pattern.

2. Fold the fabric and pin the pattern to the fabric through both layers.

3. Cut carefully around the pattern edges, and remove pins and pattern. You will have two identical pieces of fabric—a front and a back.

Make the dress

1. With right sides together, place the front and back of the dress directly on top of each other. Pin the shoulder and side seams together.

2. Sew the shoulder and side seams ⅛ inch in from the edge.

3. Turn the dress right side out and at the center of the back neckline cut a small slit (about 1 inches long) so that the dress will fit over the doll's head.

Finish the dress

Try the dress on your doll or dummy. If you want the dress to be shorter, fold the bottom of the dress up ½ inch (or more) toward the wrong side and hem with a straight stitch.

VARIATION

Tunic

This dress can easily be turned into a tunic-style shirt/dress. Follow the directions for the Shift Dress, but when sewing the side seams stop stitching 1½ inches from the bottom on each side. Fold under the raw side edges ⅛ inch toward the wrong side and sew. (See page 23.) Then turn the bottom edge under ¼ inch and hem. Cut 1¼-inch slit at the front center neck. It's fun to decorate your

tunic with embroidery (see page 62). Making small stitches along the tunic bottom and neckline looks great, or try embroidering flowers or letters.

Level: VARIATION
Challenge Shift Dress

An easy way to get rid of raw edges, like those at the neck and arms of the Summer Shift Dress, is to add a lining. And there's a hidden bonus—our Challenge Shift Dress is reversible! You'll need two different fabrics (one for the outside dress, the other for the inside dress), each piece approximately 7-inches by 10-inches, the Summer Shift Dress pattern, tracing paper, a ruler, and a pencil.

1. Place a piece of tracing paper on top of the Summer Shift Dress pattern. Using your ruler and following the shape of the pattern, draw a line around the outside of the pattern to make it ⅛ inch larger all around, except at the bottom. For the curves,

measure ⅛ inch outside the original line in several spots, and mark each spot with a dot. Connect the dots to re-create the curved pattern line.

2. Cut out the new pattern you've drawn.

3. Fold the outside dress fabric in half with right sides together, and pin the new pattern piece through both layers. Cut around the pattern edges. Remove pins and pattern. Repeat for inside dress fabric. You should have four dress pieces, a front and a back each for the outside dress and the inside dress.

4. With right sides together, place the front of the outside dress directly on top of the front of the inside dress. Pin and sew around the arm, shoulder, and neck seams, ⅛ inch in from the edge, leaving the rest of the dress open. Repeat for back dress pieces of each fabric.

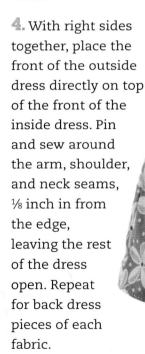

This shift is reversible—two dresses for the work of one.

5. Match up side seams of the outside fabric, right sides together. Sew side seam, ¼ inch in from the edge. Repeat for side seams of inside fabric.

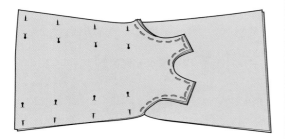

6. Clip along the curves (see page 24) at the neck and arm openings and at the shoulder corners, being careful not to cut the line of stitching. Turn neck and shoulder seams right side out.

Use a pencil to push out the corners and press with an iron. Flip outside dress over inside dress. All your seams should "disappear" to the inside and you'll have a reversible dress.

7. For the hem, fold the inside and outside dress fabric toward the wrong side, sandwiching the two seam allowances. Sew the layers together at the bottom. Try on doll or dummy and sew on snaps or Velcro at the shoulders.

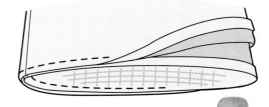

Change It Up: Make a Different Pattern

Ever look at a dress in the store and say it would be perfect if only you could change one thing? The good news is, changes are easy once you have a pattern that fits—and this goes for yourself or your doll.

1. Place tracing paper on top of the original pattern. Draw a new shape over the old. For our example, I tried out a shorter Summer Shift Dress with a scoop neck.

2. When you're happy with your drawing, cut out the new pattern and experiment, using inexpensive fabric like muslin or paper towels (see page 19). Sometimes you'll have to go back to the drawing board and revise your drawing. The dressmaker dummy will really come in handy here for trying on—and retrying—your new designs until they're perfect.

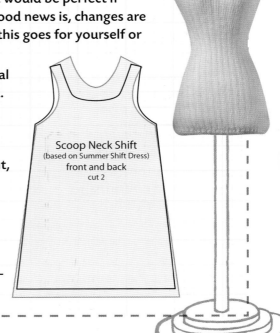

Scoop Neck Shift
(based on Summer Shift Dress)
front and back
cut 2

Little Black Dress

Level: 🕴🕴

Horrified by the gaudy array of colors worn by women at parties, designer Coco Chanel decided that we would be more dignified in black and in the 1920s introduced the now famous little black dress. She was right! Today just about every woman in the Western world has at least one—it's easy to wear, easy to dress up or down depending on the occasion, and above all, easy to look good in. Our version is inspired by the simple black sheath Audrey Hepburn wore in *Breakfast at Tiffany's*. But there's no rule that says it must be black, so make it silver, gold, red, or any color you like.

Supplies

* **7-inch by 7-inch piece of lightweight wool or synthetic fabric that won't unravel (like the synthetic fabric used to make sports uniforms), or even T-shirt fabric**
* **Scissors**
* **Ruler**
* **Needle and thread**
* **Small piece of Velcro**

PATTERN included

Cut the fabric

1. Copy or trace the pattern pieces on page 127 for the front and back of the dress. Cut out the paper patterns.

2. Fold the fabric in half. Pin the front pattern piece to the fabric along the fold through both layers of fabric. Pin the back pattern piece through both layers of fabric, but not on the fold.

3. Cut carefully around the pattern edges, and remove pins and pattern. You will have one front and two back pieces.

Make the dress

1. With right sides together, place the two back pieces on top of the front, matching the shoulders and sides, and pin in place. Sew shoulder and side seams ⅛ inch in from the edge.

2. Turn right side out and try on the dummy. Sew on a few tiny pieces of Velcro or snaps along the center back opening to close the dress, leaving 1 inch or so open at the bottom.

The Perfect Little Dress

Slim and sophisticated, effortless and elegant, Audrey Hepburn was a lot like the little black dress itself. She looked great but never like she was trying too hard. One of the most famous little black dresses (right) was designed for her role in the film *Breakfast at Tiffany's* by French designer Hubert de Givenchy. The Givenchy creation was the perfect dress, the scene outside Tiffany's windows was the perfect fashion moment in film, and Audrey, in her role as Holly Golightly, was the perfect new icon: the fashion-forward New York City single girl.

Ruffled Slip Dress

Level: ▮▮▮

Like T-shirts and tank tops, slip dresses are another case of underwear turning into outerwear. When I was a kid, my mom still thought it was a good idea to wear a slip under any and every skirt or dress. I said no. But as a dress, I say yes! Short or long, silky and slinky, slips make great simple dresses, and the ruffles make it festive! Or make a slip nightie from a piece of cozy flannel.

Supplies

* **12-inch by 6-inch piece of woven cotton or silk fabric (or flannel for a nightie) for the dress**
* **24-inch by 4-inch piece of woven cotton or silk fabric for the ruffles**
* **6-inch piece of ⅛-inch-wide ribbon**
* **Ruler**
* **Scissors**
* **Iron (optional)**
* **Needle and thread**

PATTERN
included

Cut the pattern pieces from the fabric

1. Copy or trace the pattern pieces on pages 122–123 for the dress front and the dress back. For the ruffle, make a paper pattern 22-inches by 1½-inches. Cut out paper patterns.

2. Fold the dress fabric in half and pin the dress front and back pattern pieces to the fabric on the fold. Fold the ruffle fabric in half and pin the ruffle pattern to it. Cut carefully around the pattern edges, and remove pins and patterns. You will have a front and back of the dress and two ruffles.

Make the dress

1. Fold under ⅛ inch at the dress front neck and armholes toward the wrong side of the fabric. The neck is slightly curved, so clip along the raw edge (see page 24). Pin or press with an iron and stitch along the arms and neck.

2. Repeat step 1 for the top of the dress back. Remove pins from dress front and dress back after sewing.

3. With right sides of fabric together, pin the front and back of dress together along the side seams. Sew the side seams ⅛ inch in from edge.

Finish the dress

1. Cut two 3-inch pieces of skinny (about ⅛-inch) ribbon for the straps. Pin one strap to the inside of the dress front and stitch in place. Repeat for second strap.

2. Try the dress on the dummy. Tie the straps around the neck or tuck the straps into the back of the dress and pin in place—either straight or crossed like an X. Sew to secure. Trim off excess strap if necessary.

3. To attach the ruffles, leave the dress on the dummy. Starting on one side, line up the top of the bottom ruffle 1 inch up from the bottom of the dress, with the wrong side of the ruffle facing the right side of the dress. Pin the ruffle in place, folding as you go to create the ruffled look. Stitch ruffle along the top with dress still on the dummy, removing pins as you sew. Repeat for top

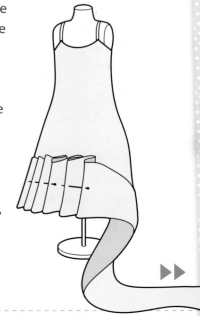

ruffle, pinning and sewing it about ½ inch up from bottom ruffle.

Note: Backstitch every few stitches to keep the bottom of the dress from gathering along with the ruffle, and don't worry if your ruffles look a bit uneven—that's part of the charm!

VARIATION
Out of Ribbon?
Cut and sew a set of fabric straps.

1. Make a paper pattern 3-inches by ½-inch.

2. Fold the fabric in half and pin the strap pattern to the fabric. Cut carefully around the pattern edges, and remove pins and patterns. You will have two straps.

3. Fold each strap in thirds lengthwise, folding toward the wrong side of the fabric and overlapping. Sew a line of stitching down the center of each strap. Pin and stitch in place.

VARIATION
Too Ruffly?
Add a layer or two of lace instead. Turn the fabric under ¼ inch at the bottom to make a hem and pin or press with an iron. Before you stitch, use the same pins to attach a 10-inch piece of lace along the hem. Sew the hem, stitching through the lace as you go.

See how the same pattern can give two very different looks.

Princess Party Dress

Level: ♟♟♟

When you think of a ball gown, what comes to mind? I've always thought of a colorful satiny dress with a fitted bodice and a great big, poufy skirt. The basic shape of the ball gown really hasn't changed much since Cinderella missed the last pumpkin carriage home. Sometimes, skirts were so full that two girls could barely get close enough to tell a secret! Our party dress can be dressed up in a shimmery silk, or dressed down in a floral print.

Make a purse out of paper.

Supplies

* **Less than ¼ yard of silk taffeta or woven cotton**
* **Newsprint, tracing paper, or wrapping paper for the pattern**
* **Ruler**
* **Scissors**
* **Needle and thread**
* **Tailor's chalk (or sharp pencil)**
* **Small piece of Velcro**

PATTERN included

Make it shorter or add some ruffles!

Make the pattern pieces and cut the fabric

1. Copy or trace the pattern on page 120 for the bodice. Make your own paper pattern for the skirt, an 18-inch by 8-inch rectangle on newsprint. Try a 15-inch by 5-inch rectangle for a shorter skirt. Cut out both paper patterns.

2. With right sides together, fold a small piece of the fabric in half. Pin the long edge of the bodice pattern along the fold as indicated on the pattern. Cut carefully around the pattern edges, and remove pins and pattern. Put pattern aside to use in bodice section.

3. Pin the skirt pattern to the fabric and cut around the pattern edges.

Make the bodice

1. Keep the bodice folded with right sides together, pin along the short sides, and stitch a seam ¼ inch in from the edge on both sides. Remove the pins. Your bodice should be a double layer with one long side open.

2. Turn the bodice right side out so the seam allowances are on the inside, and gently push out the corners with a pencil so they're square.

3. On the bodice paper pattern, cut out the dart triangles as marked and throw away the triangles. Center the pattern on top of bodice and, using

tailor's chalk, trace the triangular shapes (or darts) onto the fabric.

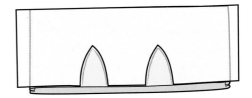

4. Fold each dart matching the chalk lines, being sure to fold the double layer of the bodice fabric into each dart. Pin and then sew a line of straight stitching along the chalk dart lines beginning at the raw edge and ending at the top point of each dart.

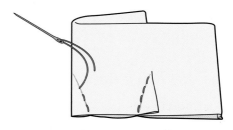

Gather the skirt

1. Using a ruler and chalk, measure along one long edge of the skirt to divide it into quarters. Mark the ¼, ½, and ¾ points.

2. Mark with chalk the ¼, ½, and ¾ points along the bottom edge of the bodice.

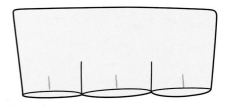

3. Sew a line of basting stitches (see page 23) along the long edge of the skirt. With right sides together, pin the top of the skirt to the bottom of the bodice, so the sides of the bodice are ¼ inch in from the skirt edge on both sides. Match up and pin at the chalk marks on the bodice and the skirt.

4. Pull both ends of the basting thread to gather the skirt until it is the same width as the bodice. Use your fingers to spread the gathers evenly, then pin the skirt to the bodice.

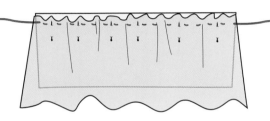

5. Sew a line of stitching ¼ inch in from the top edge. You want this to be a strong seam, so make your stitches as small as possible, and sew a backstitch (see page 24) every few stitches. Remove pins and basting stitches.

Finish the dress

1. With right sides together, fold the dress in half and pin the edges of the skirt together. Beginning at the bottom of the skirt, sew ¼ inch in from the edge and stop 1 inch before you reach the bodice.

2. At the top of the skirt, fold under the raw edges of the open seam and sew with a straight stitch close to the fold. (See page 25, Finishing Edges.)

3. Make the hem. Fold up ½ inch at bottom of dress toward the wrong side and stitch close to the edge.

4. Try the dress on a doll or the dummy. With chalk or a pin, mark the placement of Velcro or small snap closures at the waist. Remove dress, and sew on closures. (See Fasten, page 24.)

Add a Ruffle!

Follow Princess Party Dress instructions for making the bodice. Make a 15-inch by 5¾-inch paper pattern for the skirt and a 30-inch by 2¼-inch paper pattern for the ruffle. Pin patterns to fabric and cut around edges. Remove pins and patterns. Sew basting stitches along one long side of the ruffle. Attach ruffle to the bottom of the skirt by following the steps in Gather the skirt (page 76). Follow Finish the dress instructions for the Princess Party Dress, but instead of Step 3, make a ¼-inch hem along the bottom of the ruffle.

Here Comes the Bride

What does the fashion runway have in common with a walk down the aisle? Answer: the wedding dress. It's a tradition to end every fashion collection with the designer's showstopping wedding dress design. Just when it seemed like every single variation of the white wedding dress had been done, designers take the challenge one step further. Nowadays, we see runway wedding dresses made of paper and white plastic garbage bags. See if you can come up with something new. Ours is made from a white T-shirt and rows and rows of mismatched lace trim. To make our wedding dress, follow the Princess Party Dress instructions but use white cotton jersey fabric. Before attaching the skirt to the bodice, pin and sew 18-inch-long pieces of lace onto the skirt one on top of the other, overlapping each piece of lace about ⅛ inch. Sew a small piece of lace to the top of the bodice. Make a veil by cutting a 14-inch circle of white tulle netting, and pinning it to the doll's hair.

When it comes to wedding dresses, most people believe the more fabric the better.

CHAPTER 9

Jackets

S weaters may make you feel relaxed and homey, but jackets make you look and feel dressed and ready to face the world. Jackets are short or long, boxy or tailored, hooded, wooly, fuzzy, with a collar or collarless like the mod jackets that took America by storm when the Beatles invaded our shores. Don't be scared—our jacket projects look sophisticated, but they are really very easy to make.

PROJECTS

- Little Red Cape, *p. 80*
- Coco Jacket, *p. 82*
- Duffle Coat, *p. 84*

Little Red Cape

Level: 🔴🔴

This cape project was inspired by the Space Age capes that French designer André Courrèges made in the 1960s. It also reminds me of Little Red Riding Hood skipping through the forest to visit her grandmother, never suspecting that she will soon meet up with the Big, Bad Wolf. I think you'll have better luck. And of course, the cape doesn't have to be red.

Supplies

* **8-inch by 8-inch piece of stretchy fabric, like cotton jersey, lightweight Polarfleece, or a felted piece of an old sweater**
* **Scissors**
* **Ruler**
* **Needle and thread**
* **Tailor's chalk**

PATTERN included

Seams on the outside are very hip and modern.

Cut the fabric

1. Copy or trace cape, hood, and pocket pattern pieces on page 118. Cut out paper patterns, making sure to mark the armhole slit in the cape and the pocket.

2. Fold the fabric in half, with wrong sides together, and pin the pattern pieces to the fabric through both layers, being sure the top of the hood is on the fold as marked on the pattern.

3. Carefully cut around the pattern edges. Mark with chalk and cut the slits for the armholes, remove pins and patterns. You should have two cape pieces, one hood, and two circle pockets.

Making the cape

Note: For a hip look, I decided to let the seams show on the outside and so I sewed the fabric wrong sides together.

1. With wrong sides together, pin the cape body pieces together at the back. Sew the back seam ⅛ inch in from the edge. (If you prefer, sew the fabric with right sides together, and leave the seams on the inside.)

2. Leaving the hood fabric folded with wrong sides together, sew the back seam of the hood ⅛ inch in from the edge.

3. With wrong sides together, line up the back seam of the hood with the back seam of the cape. Pin the edge of the hood to the neckline edge of the back of the cape. Sew ⅛ inch in from the edge.

4. With wrong sides together, sew the front seam ⅛ inch in from the edge.

5. Pin circle pockets to the cape armholes, lining up the cuts in the circles with the slits in the cape. Sew around the outside of each circle with a straight stitch to attach them to the cape.

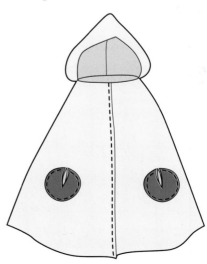

Coco Jacket

Level: 👗👗

After sewing a few of these jackets, I am certain that influential fashion designer Coco Chanel got the idea for her famous, boxy, menswear-inspired Chanel jacket from the simple, traditional Austrian boiled wool jackets—like those worn by the von Trapp family in *The Sound of Music*. This project is quick and easy, so you'll have time left to decorate it—either with trim for a classic Chanel look or with appliquéd birds or flowers that will make you feel like yodeling on a mountaintop. Pair it with the Straight Mod Mini Skirt to make a Chanel-style suit.

For a matching skirt, see Mod Mini 1–2–3 Skirt on page 52.

Supplies

* **Approximately 9-inch by 9-inch piece of felt, wool, velour, or sweatshirt material**
* **Ruler**
* **Needle and thread**
* **Scissors**
* **Tailor's chalk**

PATTERN included

Note: This jacket has lots of raw, unhemmed edges, so choose a fabric that won't unravel too much or fringe the edge.

Cut the fabric

1. Copy or trace the jacket and pocket patterns on page 128. Cut out the paper patterns.

2. Fold fabric in half with right sides together. Pin patterns to the fabric, lining up the shoulder with the fold. Mark the position of the pocket.

3. Cut carefully around the pattern edges, and remove pins and pattern. You will have one jacket piece and one pocket piece.

Make the jacket

1. Open up the jacket piece and, only on the front, cut a straight line up the center. This makes two jacket fronts that are attached to the back at the shoulder.

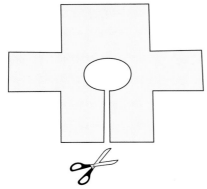

2. With right sides together and jacket folded at the shoulders, pin sleeves and side seams, and sew ⅛ inch in from the edge. If you like, don't sew all the way to the end of the sleeves and roll them up.

Finish the jacket

1. Turn jacket right side out. Pin pocket in place on right front of the jacket, as marked. Then sew around the sides and bottom of the pocket close to the edge, leaving the top open.

2. Use your creativity to decorate the jacket with appliqué or embroidery (see pages 62 and 86), or sew rick rack around the edges of the jacket. If you decorate the pocket, do that before sewing it on.

Making Felt

Find a sweater someone in your family has outgrown or buy an inexpensive one at your local thrift store. Make sure the sweater is 100 percent wool. Run the sweater through a hot water wash with laundry detergent and dry in a regular cycle. The microscopic hooks in the wool fibers grab one another and come closer together with water, heat, and agitation. If necessary, repeat the process until you have a dense fabric that no longer unravels when cut. Your felted fabric works well for any projects in this chapter.

Duffle Coat

Level: ♟♟

Tie on a Classic Silk Scarf, page 88.

Who doesn't love a duffle coat? They've been worn by everyone from musicians Bing Crosby and Lily Allen, and members of the band Oasis, to Paddington Bear. The hooded woolen duffle coat owes its popularity to the British Royal Navy in WWI—the wool was warm and the toggle buttons were easy to fasten while wearing gloves in the cold sea air. After the war, these practical coats were available at army-navy surplus stores and spread in popularity.

Drawstring Picnic Skirt, see page 54

Supplies

* **Approximately 11-inch by 16-inch piece of felt or wool fabric**
* **Scissors**
* **Ruler**
* **Needle and thread**

PATTERN included

Cut the fabric

1. Copy or trace the coat, hood, and pocket patterns on page 129. Cut out paper patterns.

2. Fold the fabric in half with right sides together and pin pattern pieces to the fabric, lining up the shoulder and the top of the hood on the fold.

3. Cut carefully around the edges, and remove pins and patterns. You will have a body, a hood, and two pockets.

Make the coat

1. Open up the coat piece and cut a straight line up the center front. (See illustration on page 83.) You'll have two coat fronts attached to the back at the shoulders.

2. With right sides together, sew the back hood seam. Turn right side out.

3. With right sides together, pin the bottom raw edge of the hood to the back neckline edge of the coat. Sew the hood to the coat.

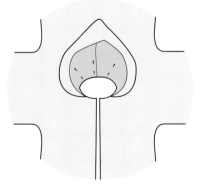

4. With right sides together, fold the coat at the shoulders. Pin sleeve and side seams, and sew seams ⅛ inch in from the edge. Leave ½ inch open at the end of each sleeve and 1 inch open at the bottom of each side.

Finish the coat

1. Line up pockets so they're even, then pin one pocket to each side of the front of the coat. Sew around the sides and bottom of each pocket with a straight stitch close to the edge. The top of the pocket will be open.

2. Roll up sleeves. For bottom side slits, turn raw edges under ⅛ inch toward the wrong side, pin, and sew close to the fold. (See page 23.)

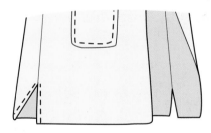

VARIATION
Add a collar instead of a hood

1. Make a rectangular paper pattern 1½-inches by 4¾-inches. Cut out paper pattern. Pin pattern to fabric and carefully cut around pattern edges.

2. With the coat inside out, pin the right side of the collar to the wrong

side (or inside) of the neckline of the coat. With a straight stitch, sew ⅛ inch in from the edge. Flip the collar over to the outside of the coat.

3. To help the collar lie flat, press the neckline seam toward the collar and stitch through the seam allowance and collar.

Appliqué

Here's a fun and easy way to decorate your clothes. To appliqué, you cut out shapes from one fabric and sew (or apply) those shapes onto another fabric. Make an allover pattern—repeating leaves, flowers, circles—or appliqué a single figure or a scene from a favorite story. Try cutting your shapes from felt or cotton jersey fabric, which won't unravel.

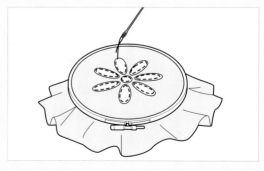

SUPPLIES

* *Fabric (felt or cotton jersey in different colors)*
* *Chalk or pencil*
* *Scissors*
* *Needle*
* *Embroidery thread or sewing thread*
* *Embroidery hoop (optional)*

1. Sketch your design directly on the fabric or cut out a drawing from a magazine and trace it on the fabric with chalk or pencil.

Feel free to use more than one color appliqué fabric in your design, for example, white fabric for a house, red for the door, and yellow for the windows.

2. Cut out the appliqué pieces.

3. If you like, put the fabric you want to decorate in the embroidery hoop. The hoop keeps the fabric flat and taut, and makes it easier to sew on your appliqué designs.

4. Pin appliqué pieces to your fabric. Attach the design pieces in place by sewing close to their cut edges.

Accessories

For the past couple of years, I've watched as my daughter has developed a flair for accessories. It all started after seeing some Audrey Hepburn movies—think silk scarves, dark sunglasses, large pearls, and even larger hats. Now not a day goes by when my daughter doesn't wear a pair of funky-colored tights, wrap a scarf around her neck, or layer what looks like one outfit over another (but winds up looking supercute).

Classic Silk Scarf

Level:

The silk scarf is probably the most important fashion accessory of all time. Screen-printed Hermès scarves are worn by women around the world from the Queen of England to Sarah Jessica Parker. There are nearly as many ways to tie a scarf as there are beautiful patterns. Try tying one around the waist as a belt, or fold it diagonally and tie it around the body for a cute little top.

Make the pattern and cut the fabric

1. Measure and mark a paper pattern of a 6½-inch square. Cut out paper pattern.

2. Pin the pattern to fabric. Cut around the pattern edges, and remove pins and pattern.

Finish scarf

1. Hem the raw edges of the square by folding or rolling the fabric two times, ⅛ inch each, toward the wrong side and pin or press. Stitch around all the edges.

2. Fold the scarf into a triangle and tie around neck, head, waist, or body.

Supplies

* **7-inch by 7-inch square piece of patterned lightweight silk or cotton**
* **Newsprint or tracing paper, for the pattern**
* **Ruler**
* **Scissors**
* **Needle and thread**

Make YOUR OWN Pattern

Knee Socks

Level:

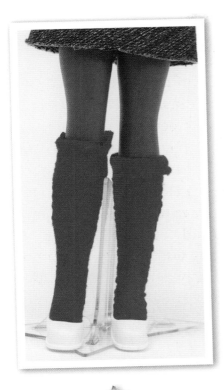

Socks absorb sweat, protect your feet and legs, and sometimes even dress up your outfit. Long, tall socks remind you to stand up straight! Make these adorable socks in lots of colors. The taller thigh highs double as tights.

Make It

Cut the fabric

1. Decide between knee socks and thigh highs and copy or trace the pattern on page 122. Cut out.

2. Tug on the fabric to find out which way stretches the most (see page 31). Fold the fabric in half with right sides together and pin the pattern to fabric through both layers so the most stretch follows the direction indicated by the arrows on the pattern.

3. Cut carefully around the pattern edges, and remove pins and pattern. Repeat steps 2 and 3. You should now have four pieces, enough to make two socks.

Make the socks

1. With right sides still together, pin two of the pieces together. Stitch around three sides of the sock ⅛ inch in from the edge. Leave the top open. Repeat for other sock.

Supplies

* 6-inch by 6-inch piece of cotton jersey or a piece of an old T-shirt
* Ruler
* Scissors
* Needle and thread

PATTERN included

Bathing Suit

Level: 🗍

Way back in the 1970s, a poster of a beautiful woman in a red swimsuit sold 12 million copies and graced the walls of nearly every teenaged boy in America. The woman was Farrah Fawcett, model and soon-to-be star of the TV series *Charlie's Angels,* and memory of her famous red swimsuit inspired this supercute project.

Supplies

* **Approximately 4½-inch by 8-inch piece of cotton jersey or piece cut from an old T-shirt**
* **Newsprint, tracing paper, or wrapping paper for the pattern**
* **Ruler**
* **Scissors**
* **Needle and thread**

Make YOUR OWN Pattern

Make the pattern and cut the fabric

1. Make one paper pattern 4¼-inches by 3½-inches for the bathing suit and one paper pattern ¼-inch by 8-inches for the strap. Cut out paper patterns.

2. Tug on the fabric to see which way the fabric stretches the most. Pin the pattern to the fabric, with the most stretch going along the longer side. Cut carefully around the pattern edges, and remove pins and pattern.

3. Pin the strap pattern to the fabric with the most stretch going along the long side. Cut around the pattern edges, remove pins and pattern.

Make the bathing suit

1. With right sides together, fold bathing suit fabric in half so the shorter sides meet and sew ⅛ inch in from the edge, for the back seam. You will have a tube.

2. With right sides still together, turn the tube so the seam is in the center back. Sew a ½-inch line of stitching at the center of one open side to create the

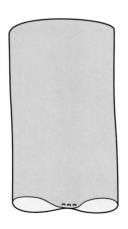

crotch, and leave holes for the legs. Turn bathing suit right side out.

Finish the bathing suit

1. Try on doll (this bathing suit won't fit on the dummy because she doesn't have legs!) and ⅛ inch down from top edge, make a ½-inch-long vertical stitch at the center front; this becomes the bodice. Pull the stitch tight to gather fabric at the bustline. Stitch again over the first stitch to reinforce.

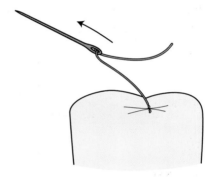

2. Fold the strap in half so it measures ¼-inch by 4-inches. Pin the fold to the center of the bodice on the inside of the top edge. Sew the strap to the bathing suit near the bodice tuck. Put suit on doll and tie the ends of the strap in a bow around her neck.

Belt

Level: 🎀

Belts can be useful; they can help you carry your tools if you're building a house or saving the world (think Batman), they can hold up your pants if they're hand-me-downs from your big sister, and most important, they can give an outfit that final something that it needs to be right (think a perfect belted dress or a jacket held together by a belt with a large decorative buckle).

So cool! I want one.

Jacket looks glam with a buckle.

Tank Dress, see page 39

Supplies

* **¼-inch by 7-inch piece of leather (fake or real)**
* **Ruler**
* **Scissors**
* **Washer from the hardware store with a center hole slightly larger than ¼ inch in diameter. (I used one that was ¾-inch-wide.)**
* **Embroidery needle and embroidery thread**

Make the belt

1. Cut off 6 inches of the 7-inch-long piece of leather.

2. Thread one end of the leather through the washer, fold ½ inch of the end over the washer to the other side and using embroidery thread and straight stitches, sew end in place to hold. The washer is the belt buckle.

3. To make the belt loop, fold the remaining 1-inch piece of leather around the belt near the buckle and overlap the ends. With straight stitches and embroidery thread, sew the ends together to hold in place.

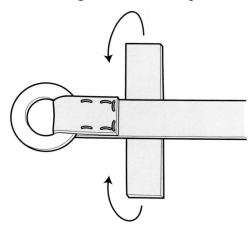

4. Wrap belt around doll's waist, thread the loose end through the washer buckle and through the belt loop.

VARIATION

Fabric Belt

If you can't find leather, you can make a belt out of fabric. If you're using lightweight fabric, start with a piece that's ¾-inch by 6-inches. If you're using heavier canvas, cut a piece that's ½-inch by 6-inches. For lightweight fabric, fold the belt in thirds overlapping top and bottom toward the wrong side of the fabric. For heavier canvas, fold it in half, so the belt measures ¼-inch-wide. Straight stitch down the center of belt through all layers. For the loop, cut a single piece of fabric ½-inch by 1-inch. Fold in half lengthwise and stitch down the center. Then follow instructions for the leather belt.

Messenger Bag

Level: 🎀🎀

When I first moved to New York, the city streets were filled with bicycle messengers with their large, rectangular bags slung over one shoulder, carrying important papers from office to office. The advent of e-mailing has meant fewer bike messengers, but the hip messenger bag still lives on.

Supplies

* **4½-inch by 5½-inch piece of felt (or other fabric that doesn't unravel)**
* **Scissors**
* **Tailor's chalk**
* **Needle and embroidery thread**
* **9-inch-long by ⅜-inch-wide piece of ribbon or twill tape for strap**
* **Ruler**
* **Small piece of Velcro**

PATTERN included

Sock Dress, see page 28

Cut the fabric

1. Copy or trace the pattern on page 124. Cut out paper pattern.

2. Pin the pattern to fabric. Cut carefully around the pattern edges, and remove pins but do not remove the pattern. One fold at a time, fold the pattern along each fold, using tailor's chalk to draw the fold lines on the fabric as you fold the pattern.

Make the bag

1. Referring to the pattern, match up sections A and B and pin the side seams of the bag. Starting at one corner where the A sections meet, sew side seams using embroidery thread, keeping the line of stitching as close to the edge as possible.

2. When you get to the flap, continue stitching along the flap even though you are not attaching it to another piece of fabric, and continue stitching around until you sew sections A and B together on the other side of the bag.

Finish the bag

1. Cut the piece of ribbon or twill tape. Pin and sew to the sides of bag, about ½ inch from the top.

2. Fold down flap and sew a snap or a small piece of Velcro on the inside center of the flap to keep the bag closed.

VARIATION

For a smaller handbag-sized version of the messenger bag, use the Clutch Handbag pattern on page 125 and follow the Messenger Bag instructions. Add a strap or just tuck it under the arm.

flap

fold

Messenger Bag

cut 1   B

fold

A

fold   A

front fold   front fold   B

A smaller messenger bag makes a perfect handbag.

Backpack

Level: 👗👗👗

You know from schlepping your heavy school bag that backpacks spread out the load and make it easier to carry lots of books. And you most likely also know that the humble backpack can be a very stylish accessory when it wants to be. So make it out of cool fabric; add appliqué and pimp your pack.

Make stitching in a contrasting color.

For Challenge T-Shirt, see page 42

Supplies

* **Approximately 3-inch by 9-inch piece of cotton or canvas fabric**
* **Ruler**
* **Scissors**
* **Tailor's chalk**
* **Needle and embroidery thread**
* **Small piece of Velcro**

PATTERN included

Embroidered circles are easy and fun! See page 62

Cut the fabric

1. Copy or trace the pattern for the bag on page 130. Make a paper pattern 3½-inches by ¾-inch for the straps. Cut out paper patterns.

2. Pin the bag pattern to the fabric. Cut carefully around the pattern edges. Remove pins but do not remove the pattern. Lift pattern edges and mark fold lines on the fabric edges with chalk. Use a ruler and chalk to connect the marks and draw the fold lines, as on the pattern.

3. Fold a small piece of fabric and pin the strap pattern to it. Cut carefully around the pattern edges. You should have two strap pieces and one bag piece.

Make the bag

1. At the front of the backpack, fold along the "front" fold line toward the wrong side of the fabric and press. Sew along the fold.

2. Fold along the line marked "bottom of the backpack" so the right sides of the fabric are together, and pin the sides together up to the fold line for the flap, and sew each side ⅛ inch in from the edge.

3. With the backpack still inside out, press down the bottom corners so the seam is in the center, and the bottom corner makes a triangle. Sew a line

of stitches ½ inch from the point. Cut off end of triangle ⅛ inch from line of stitching. Repeat for other bottom corner.

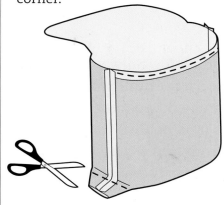

4. Turn backpack right side out. Turn under the raw edges of the flap ¼ inch toward the wrong side and pin. With straight stitches and embroidery thread, sew around the edges close to the fold.

5. Fold down flap and sew a piece of Velcro or a snap to the inside center of the flap to keep it closed.

Finish the bag

1. Fold each strap in thirds lengthwise, overlapping slightly, and pin. Sew a line of stitching down the center of each strap.

2. Pin one strap to the back of the bag so one end is at the bottom corner and the other end is at the top just below the flap ½ inch in from the edge. With embroidery thread, straight stitch in place. Repeat for other strap.

Apron

Level:

Aprons have always been practical; worn for hundreds of years by men and women alike to protect their clothes (and bodies) from all kinds of messy work, from housekeeping to woodworking to shopkeeping. Today, aprons are still practical in the kitchen—they keep food from splashing all over your clothes—but that doesn't mean they can't be fun too. Decorate your apron with appliqué, embroidery, or make one out of a fun fabric.

A pocket is a handy place to carry kitchen tools.

Supplies

* **7-inch by 9-inch piece of cotton or linen fabric**
* **Ruler**
* **Scissors**
* **Tailor's chalk**
* **Iron (optional)**
* **Needle and thread**
* **Small piece of Velcro or snap**
* **12-inch-long piece of ¼-inch-wide ribbon or twill tape for ties**

PATTERN included

Cut the fabric

1. Copy or trace the pattern pieces on page 130 for the apron and the pocket. Also make a paper pattern 4-inch by ¾-inch for the neck strap. Cut out paper patterns.

2. Fold the fabric in half and pin the apron and pocket patterns to the fabric along the fold, as indicated on the pattern. Cut carefully around the pattern edges, and remove the pins and patterns.

3. Pin the neck strap pattern to a small piece of fabric and cut carefully around the pattern edges. Remove pins and pattern.

Make the apron

1. Fold under ¼ inch toward the wrong side of fabric all the way around the apron, clipping corners on the curved parts along the apron bib (see page 24), and pin or press with an iron. Stitch close to the fold around the edge of the apron.

2. Unfold the pocket and turn under ¼ inch toward the wrong side of fabric all around the pocket and pin. Place and pin pocket on center front of apron. Stitch around sides and bottom of pocket close to edge, leaving top open.

3. Fold the neck strap in thirds lengthwise and stitch down the center of the strap. Pin one end of strap to one corner of the bib and sew in place. Sew Velcro or a snap to attach the other side of the strap to the bib.

4. Cut two 6-inch pieces of ribbon. Stitch one end of each ribbon to back corners of the apron. Try apron on dummy and tie ribbons in back.

CHAPTER 11

Make It Bigger!

Make It for Yourself!

By this point you've probably made at least a few pieces of doll-sized clothing. Maybe you've modified some of our patterns or conjured up a few original outfits. Now I bet you're itching to make some clothes for yourself. Here are a few projects to get you started. We haven't included patterns because we'll show you how to make some simple clothes by just taking a few measurements and using your math skills. Get ready to sew on a larger scale!

PROJECTS

Add a Skirt
T-Shirt Dress

Try a T-shirt in your favorite color.

Level: 🎎

This project was inspired by a dress that looked just like a T-shirt with a skirt attached. In the 1950s, when stylish women were wearing only clothes that were fitted at the waist, Balenciaga introduced the Sack Dress. His design paved the way for the loose-fitting shift dresses of the 1960s. Our dress here works equally well with a favorite old T-shirt, or a brand-new one.

Supplies

* **One loose-fitting T-shirt or tank top (to fit yourself). Depending on your size, about a yard of fabric for the skirt (cotton jersey, woven cotton, linen, silk)**
* **Iron**
* **Tailor's chalk**
* **Scissors**
* **Measuring tape**
* **Ruler**
* **Needle and thread**

Make YOUR OWN Pattern

Note: For a bargain, buy a 3-pack of boys' white T-shirts at the supermarket.

Measure yourself

1. Wash and dry the T-shirt and the fabric. Iron both, then try on the T-shirt and mark the spot 2 inches below your waist with tailor's chalk. With a ruler measure from the bottom up to the mark in several spots. Draw a line around the T-shirt, connecting the marks. Cut along the line.

2. For the skirt, use your measuring tape to take the measurements below and do the math:

Width of
the T-shirt _____" x 2 = _____"

+1" (for seam allowance) = _____" → width of skirt pattern

Length from
your waist to _____" → length of
your knee skirt pattern

These numbers are the dimensions of the front and the back of your skirt, and you'll use them to make a skirt pattern.

Cut the fabric

1. Make a rectangular paper pattern using the answers above for the length and width. Now you can figure out how much fabric you need. For example, if your rectangle measures 30-inches by

Label by Me!

Designers mark their designs with a label sewn into the garment at the neck (or waist if it's a skirt).

Cut a small square (or rectangle) of fabric—any size, about 1 inch for tiny doll clothes or 2 to 3 inches for your own clothes—and add your name, initials, or a small design. Or try a label that uses a tiny piece of a favorite fabric. Fold and press under the edges all around, pin, and sew onto the inside of the garment.

Embroider your initials on your labels.

13-inches, you'll need two times that much fabric, which would be about 26 inches long, or about ¾ of a 36-inch yard.

2. Fold the fabric in half with right sides together and pin the pattern to

the fabric. Cut carefully around the pattern edges, and remove the pins and pattern. You will now have the front and the back of the skirt.

Lucy, Emma, and Kiki trying out their new dresses.

Make the skirt

1. With right sides together, pin the front and the back of the skirt together along the short sides. Sew both side seams ½ inch in from the edge so the skirt is a tube.

2. Using a piece of chalk and a ruler, measure and mark along the entire bottom edge of the T-shirt to divide it into quarters, marking the ¼, ½, and ¾ points. Mark the top of the skirt in the same way. With a basting stitch (see page 23), sew around the top edge of the skirt with one long piece of thread.

3. With right sides together, pin the bottom of the T-shirt and the top of the skirt together, matching the side seams and the marked points. That means putting the skirt over the T-shirt, as shown, and pinning around the entire bottom of T-shirt. Pull both ends of the basting thread so the skirt gathers and is the same width as the T-shirt bottom. With your fingers, spread the gathers evenly and pin.

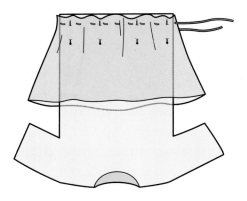

4. With a straight stitch, sew the T-shirt and skirt together ½ inch in from the edge. Don't worry too much about whether your gathers are perfectly even.

Finish the dress

1. On the inside, press the seam down toward the skirt. If you like, sew another line of stitching ¼ inch below the seam through the seam allowance and skirt to keep the seam flat.

2. Pin a ½ inch hem and try on the dress. If you'd like the skirt to be shorter, make the hem wider. Sew the hem along the raw edge.

Make a Matching Dress for Your Doll

Using the E-Z T-Shirt or the Challenge T-shirt pattern on pages 120 and 126, cut out fabric pieces for a T-shirt. Since the bottom of the T-shirt measures 2¾ inches, make a rectangle paper pattern for the skirt twice as wide, or 5½-inches by 3-inches. Fold fabric, pin pattern to fabric, and cut. You will have two skirt pieces. Follow instructions for putting together the T-shirt on page 40. Follow instructions to make the Add a Skirt T-Shirt Dress above.

Trapezoid T-Skirt

Level: 👗👗

What's more comfortable than a T-shirt? Answer: a skirt made out of T-shirts. And like a T-shirt, this T-skirt is a great blank canvas for some customizing—paint on it, appliqué it, patch it, have fun with it. If you want some decoration inspiration, check out designer (and sewer) Natalie Chanin's website (www.alabamachanin .com) and you'll see that in her hands the humble T-shirt is invited to the party.

Supplies

* **One or two T-shirts (depending on how much fabric you need for your size) or cotton jersey**
* **Newsprint, tracing paper, or wrapping paper for the pattern**
* **Measuring tape**
* **Yardstick or long straight edge**
* **Scissors**
* **Needle and thread**
* **Iron (optional)**
* **Safety pin**

Make YOUR OWN Pattern

Sew appliqué felt or cotton jersey stars onto your skirt.

Make It

Notes: Make the pattern first so you'll know what size and how many T-shirts you'll need. You can use some old T-shirts from your mom, dad, or older brother (though unless you want a two-tone skirt, choose two that are the same color) or buy yardage of cotton jersey instead.

Make the pattern

1. The pattern for this project is in the shape of a trapezoid, or a triangle with its top cut off. Begin by measuring your waist, and divide that number by four. This number will be used for the top of the trapezoid. For example, if your waist measures 24 inches, the top of the trapezoid will measure 6 inches.

2. Multiply the top number by two, to find the number for the bottom of your trapezoid. In our example above, the bottom of the trapezoid will measure 12 inches.

3. Measure the distance from your waist to the top of your knees, or wherever you'd like the skirt to end. Add 1 inch and this is the length of your pattern. For example, if the distance between your waist and your knee is 14 inches, the length of the trapezoid pattern piece should be 15 inches.

4. On a large piece of paper (newspaper works well for full-sized patterns), draw a line equal to the length of the skirt (from step 3).

5. At the top of that line, draw a line straight across that equals the measurement for the top of the trapezoid (from step 1). Make sure that the center of the top line lines up with the top of the length line.

6. Repeat at the bottom of the length line, drawing a line the size of the bottom of the trapezoid (from step 2).

7. Using your yardstick, draw a straight line from the left end of the top line to the left end of the bottom line. Repeat on the right side. Cut out the paper pattern.

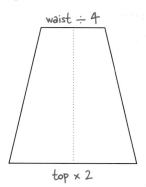

waist ÷ 4

top × 2

Cut the fabric

1. Cut off the bottom hem of the T-shirt(s) and save to use as the drawstring.

2. Lay the first T-shirt flat on a table. Pin the pattern to the T-shirt through both layers so the length of the skirt runs up and down the T-shirt.

3. Cut carefully around the pattern edges, and remove pins and pattern. Repeat this step, using an additional

T-shirt if you need one. You should have four trapezoid skirt pieces.

Make the skirt

1. With right sides of fabric together, pin the long seams of two trapezoid pieces together, and sew ¼ inch in from the edge. Repeat until all four skirt pieces are joined into a tube.

2. On the inside, press open the seam allowances with an iron or your fingers. Turn down the top of skirt 1 inch to the inside (or wrong side) of fabric. Sew ⅛ inch up from the raw edge around the top, or waistline, to create the drawstring casing.

Finish the skirt

1. For the drawstring, you'll need a piece of the bottom hem of the T-shirt that measures two times around the waist of the skirt. If one T-shirt bottom hem isn't enough, sew two pieces of T-shirt hem together to make a long enough drawstring.

Make a Matching Skirt for Your Doll

You don't need a pattern to make a matching skirt for your doll. Using the same math as above, take measurements and get started calculating, cutting, and sewing. This skirt works fine for dolls without the drawstring waistband, so you can skip that part.

2. Cut a vertical slit in the drawstring casing at the center of one of the panels. This will become the front of the skirt. Make a knot at the end of the drawstring and attach a safety pin to the knot. Thread the safety pin and drawstring into the hole in the drawstring casing and working through the fabric, use the safety pin to push and pull the drawstring through the casing and out the hole. Try on skirt and tie drawstring in a bow.

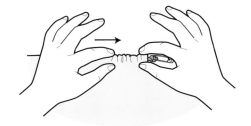

School, Beach, or Shopping Tote

Level: 👤👤

I'm sure you've noticed that reusable grocery bags are the newest in eco-chic. Reusing your bags saves trees and keeps plastic out of our landfills. Make your tote out of something sturdy so you can use it over and over again, and make it look good so you can have fun using it.

Supplies

* **30-inches by 22-inches (or just under ¾ yard) piece of cotton canvas, wool flannel, or plastic fabric**
* **Newsprint, tracing paper, or wrapping paper for the pattern**
* **Ruler**
* **Needle and embroidery thread**
* **Scissors**

Make YOUR OWN Pattern

Make the pattern and cut the fabric

1. Make two paper patterns, one 30-inches by 17-inches for the bag, and one 22-inches by 2½-inches for the straps. This will make a bag that's approximately 12-inches-wide by 12-inches-tall by 4-inches-deep. Add or subtract inches to change the size.

2. Pin the bag pattern to the fabric and cut carefully around the pattern edges. Remove pins and pattern.

3. Fold a long strip of fabric in half and pin the strap pattern to the fabric. Cut carefully around the pattern edges. You should have two strap pieces and one bag piece.

Make the bag

1. Fold the fabric in half with wrong sides of fabric together so it measures 15-inches by 17-inches. With the fold on the bottom, on each side, position one edge over the other, as shown below, overlapping the edges 1 inch and pin. With a straight stitch and using embroidery thread, stitch each side seam close to the raw edge. The bottom corners will come to a point.

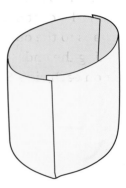

2. Stand the bag upright and press the bottom corners down. At each side, fold up the corners at the bottom of the bag so the point of the triangle meets the side seam and the bottom of the bag measures approximately 4 inches wide, and pin.

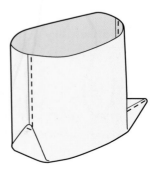

3. Sew top of each triangle to the side seam of the bag, or sew a line of stitching around all sides of the triangle.

4. Fold top edge of bag down 1 inch toward the inside of the bag, and pin. Sew around the top of the bag ¾ inch from the fold.

Finish the bag

Fold each strap in thirds lengthwise, pin, and sew down the center of each strap. Pin the straps to the outside of the bag, positioning the ends 2 inches from the center on each side. Stitch in place.

Make a Matching Bag for Your Doll

A chic tote bag for your doll is simply a smaller version of this project. You'll need a 3-inch by 7½-inch piece of cool-looking canvas or felt. Make two paper patterns: one measuring 3-inches by 6½-inches for the bag; the other 3-inches by ½-inch for the handles. Now follow steps 2 on and your doll will look as sharp as you do when you step out together.

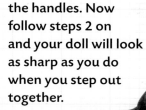

Resources

There are so many inspiring sewing and fashion books and fabric stores out there that it's hard to pick just a few to recommend, but I'll try.

SEWING BOOKS

* ***Aranzi Aronzo Fun Dolls (Let's Make Cute Stuff),*** by Aranzi Aronzo and Anne Ishii (Vertical)
* ***Kids' Embroidery: Projects for Kids of All Ages,*** by Kristin Nicholas (Stewart, Tabori & Chang)
* ***Generation T,*** by Megan Nicolay (Workman)
* ***Simple Sewing,*** by Lotta Jansdotter (Chronicle)
* ***S-E-W: Sew Everything Workshop,*** by Diana Rupp (Workman)
* ***Weekend Sewing,*** by Heather Ross (Stewart, Tabori & Chang)

FASHION BOOKS

* ***Icons of Fashion: The 20th Century,*** ed. Gerda Buxbaum (Prestel)
* ***Fashion Design,*** by Sue Jenkyn Jones (Watson-Guptill)
* ***The Fashion Book*** (Phaidon)

FAVORITE FABRIC STORES

To find a fabric store near you, look online or in the phone book.

Purl Soho
459 Broome Street
New York, NY 10013
www.purlsoho.com
Also, check out their Purl Bee blog—*www.purlbee.com*—for free patterns and projects.

Mood Designer Fabrics
Stores in New York City and Los Angeles
www.moodfabrics.com

Hancock's of Paducah
www.hancocks-paducah.com

Hart's Fabric
1620 Seabright Avenue

Fabrics and colorful embroidery thread at Purl Soho

Santa Cruz, CA 95062
www.hartsfabric.com

Sew, Mama, Sew!
www.sewmamasew.com
Check out their blog—
http://sewmamasew.com/blog2/
—for free patterns and fun projects.

Reprodepot Fabrics
www.reprodepot.com

Jo-Ann Fabric & Craft Stores
www.joann.com

FAVORITE COSTUME/ FASHION MUSEUM WEBSITES

The Costume Institute, Metropolitan Museum of Art, New York, NY
www.metmuseum.org/works_of_art/
the_costume_institute

Victoria & Albert Museum, London, England
www.vam.ac.uk/collections/fashion

Smithsonian National Museum of American History, Washington, D.C.
http://americanhistory.si.edu/collections
Click on "Clothing & Accessories"

SEWING PATTERNS

Itching for some more projects? Try some sewing patterns. Many fabric stores have books and books of clothing patterns to flip through. Or look online:

Vogue Patterns
http://voguepatterns.mccall.com

Butterick Patterns
http://butterick.mccall.com

Simplicity Patterns
www.simplicity.com

Oliver + S makes adorable patterns for kids from baby-sized to age 12.
www.oliverands.com

Folkwear Patterns
http://folkwear.com

Fashion Girls

Trace or copy our fashion girls or draw right in the book and dress them up! You might want to modify one of the designs in this book, experiment with different color combinations, or try out a completely new design of your own. Have fun!

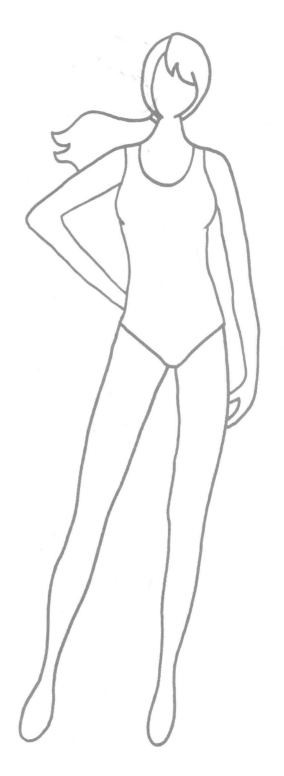

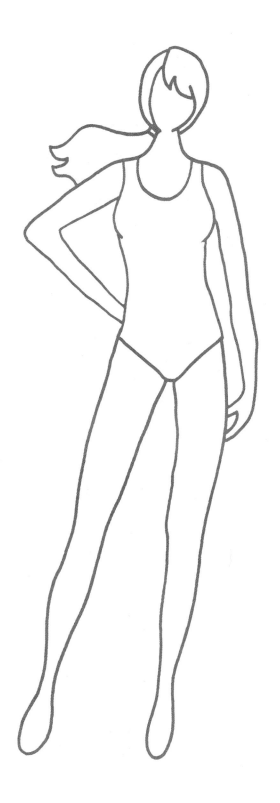

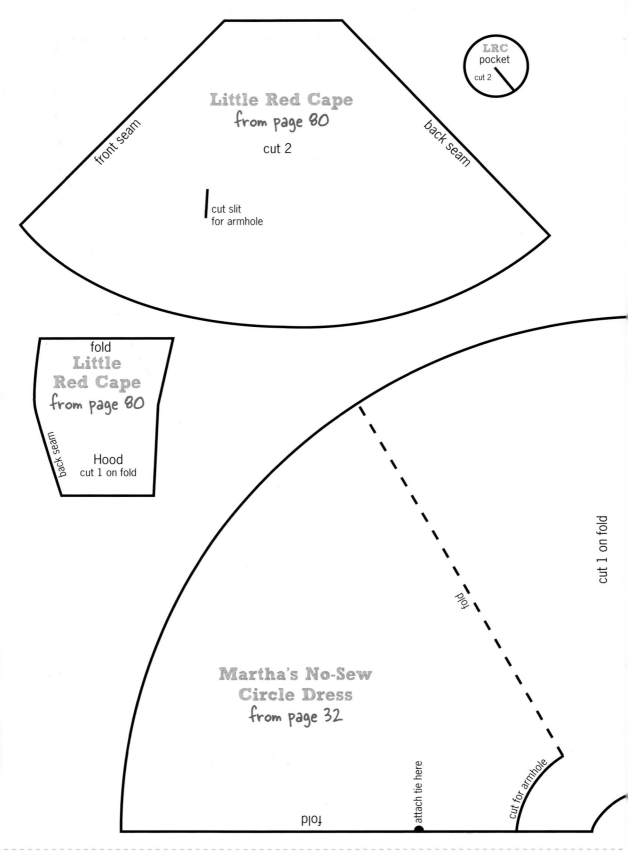

Little Red Cape
from page 80

cut 2

front seam

back seam

cut slit
for armhole

LRC
pocket
cut 2

fold
Little
Red Cape
from page 80

back seam

Hood
cut 1 on fold

Martha's No-Sew
Circle Dress
from page 32

cut 1 on fold

fold

attach tie here

cut for armhole

fold

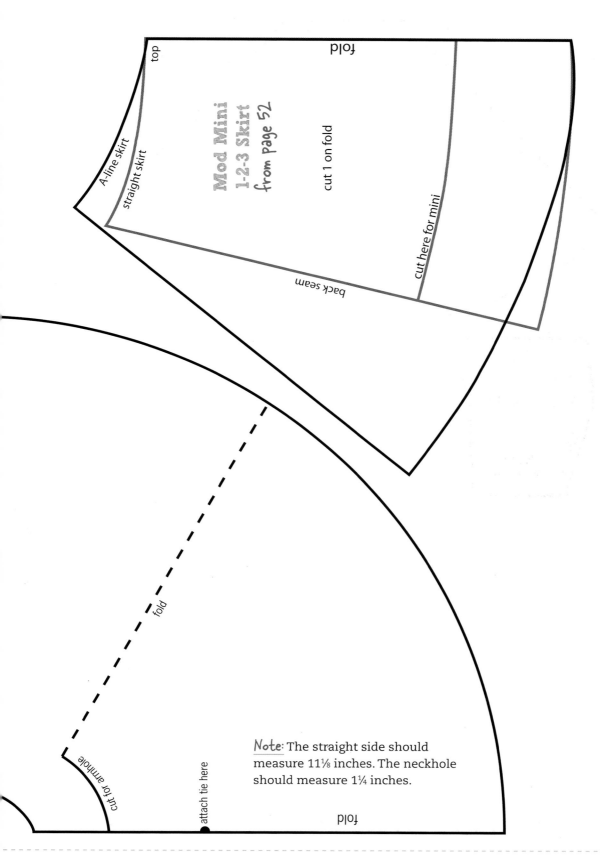

top

fold

A-line skirt

straight skirt

**Mod Mini
1-2-3 Skirt
from page 52**

cut 1 on fold

cut here for mini

back seam

fold

cut for armhole

attach tie here

Note: The straight side should measure 11⅛ inches. The neckhole should measure 1¼ inches.

fold

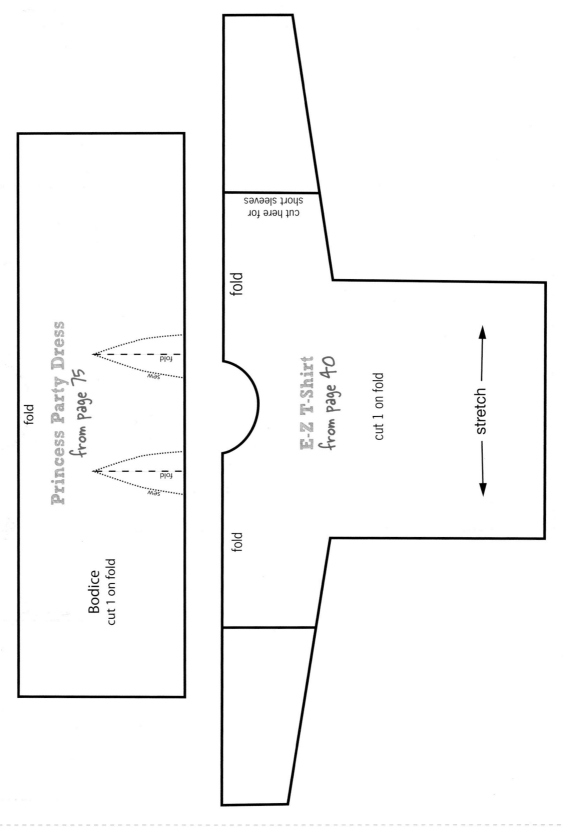

Princess Party Dress
from page 75

Bodice
cut 1 on fold

fold

fold

sew

fold

sew

E-Z T-Shirt
from page 40

cut 1 on fold

stretch

fold

fold

cut here for
short sleeves

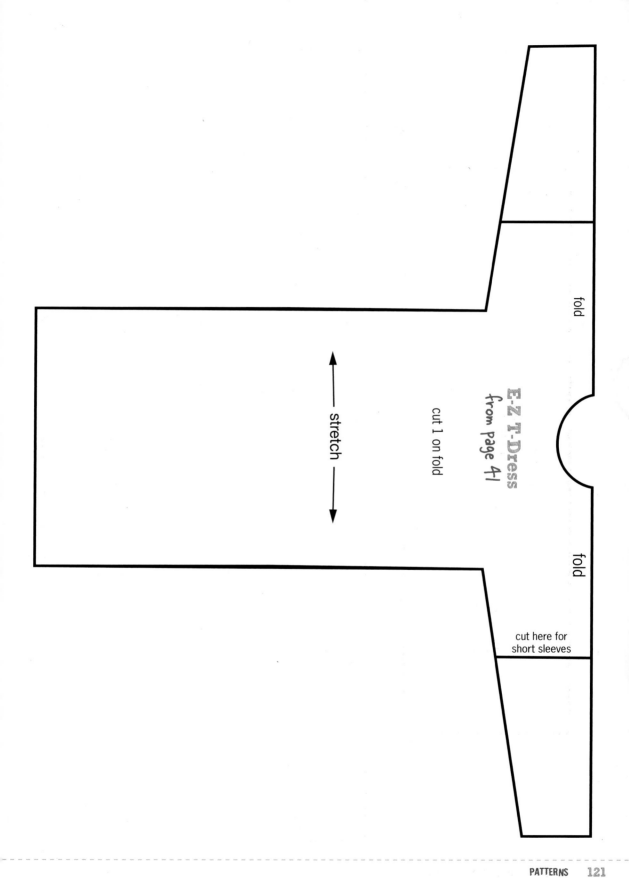

E-Z T-Dress
from page 41

cut 1 on fold

stretch

fold

fold

cut here for
short sleeves

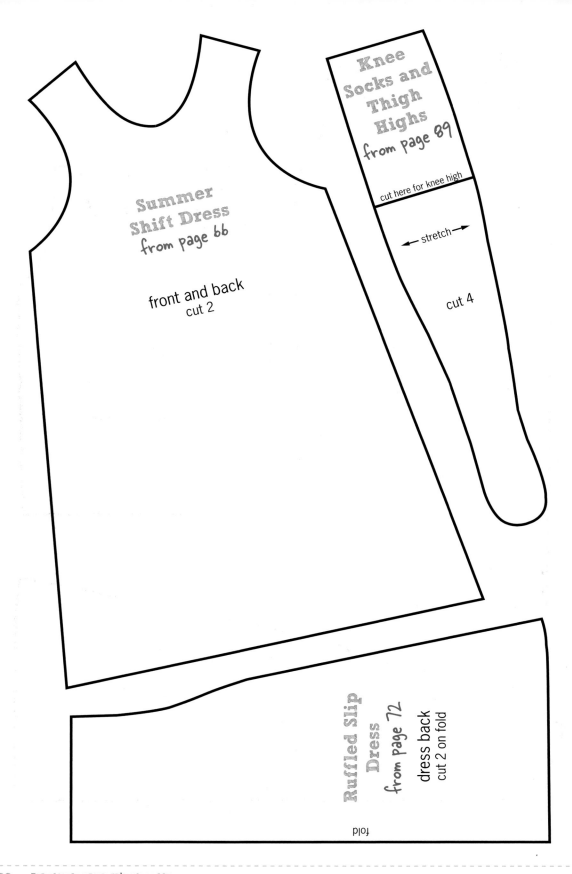

Summer Shift Dress
from page 66

front and back
cut 2

Knee Socks and Thigh Highs
from page 89

cut here for knee high

← stretch →

cut 4

Ruffled Slip Dress
from page 72

dress back
cut 2 on fold

fold

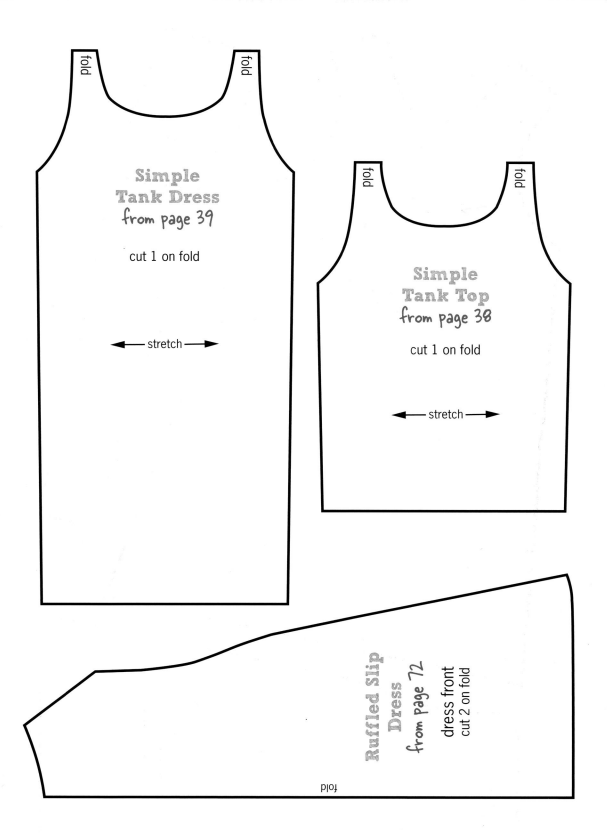

fold

fold

**Simple
Tank Dress**
from page 39

cut 1 on fold

←— stretch —→

fold

fold

**Simple
Tank Top**
from page 38

cut 1 on fold

←— stretch —→

**Ruffled Slip
Dress**
from page 72

dress front
cut 2 on fold

fold

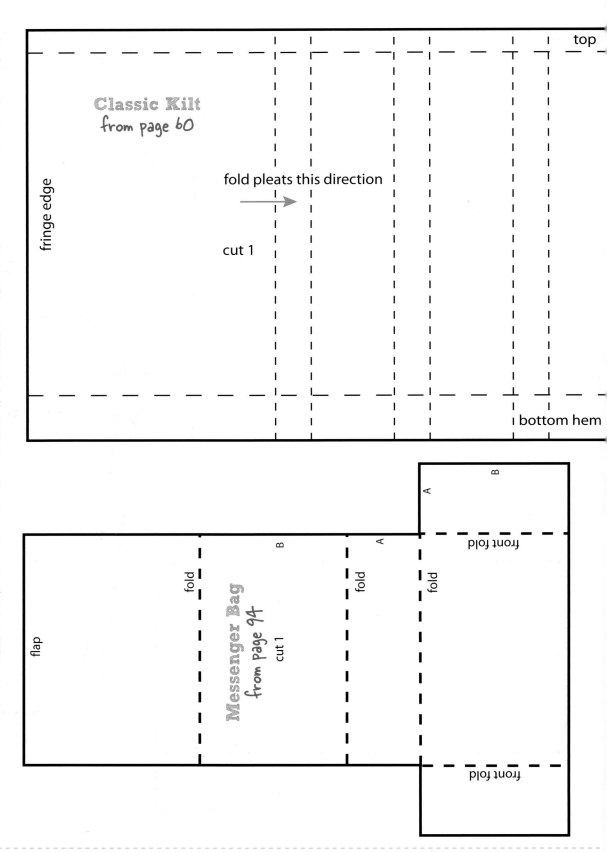

Classic Kilt
from page 60

fringe edge

top

fold pleats this direction

cut 1

bottom hem

flap

fold

Messenger Bag
from page 94

cut 1

B

A

fold

A

fold

B

front fold

front fold

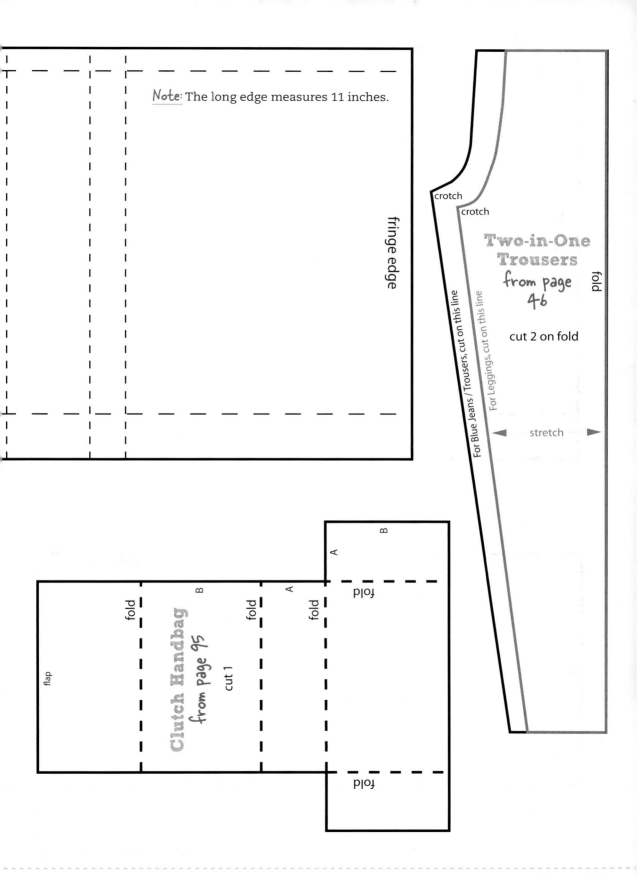

Note: The long edge measures 11 inches.

fringe edge

crotch

crotch

Two-in-One Trousers from page 46

cut 2 on fold

For Blue Jeans / Trousers, cut on this line

For Leggings, cut on this line

fold

stretch

Clutch Handbag from page 95

cut 1

flap

fold

fold

fold

fold

fold

A

B

A

B

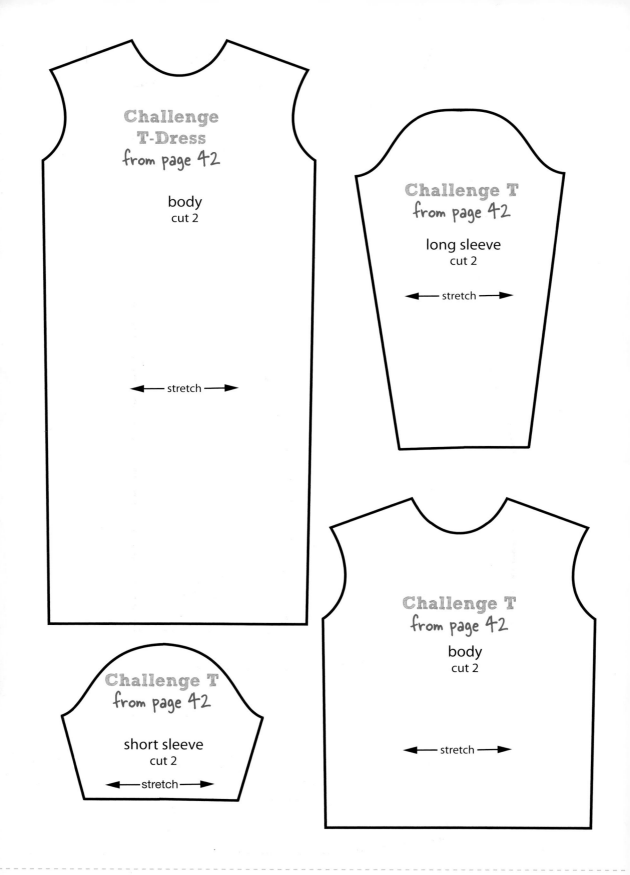

Challenge T-Dress
from page 42

body
cut 2

← stretch →

Challenge T
from page 42

long sleeve
cut 2

← stretch →

Challenge T
from page 42

body
cut 2

← stretch →

Challenge T
from page 42

short sleeve
cut 2

← stretch →

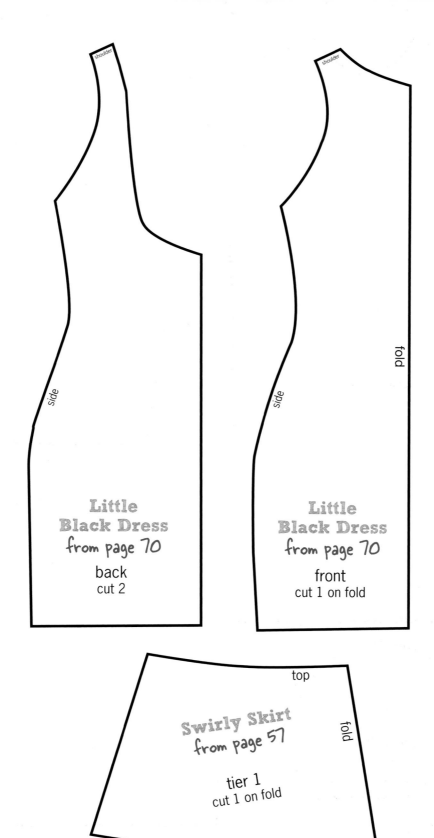

shoulder

shoulder

fold

side

side

**Little
Black Dress**
from page 70

back
cut 2

**Little
Black Dress**
from page 70

front
cut 1 on fold

top

fold

Swirly Skirt
from page 57

tier 1
cut 1 on fold

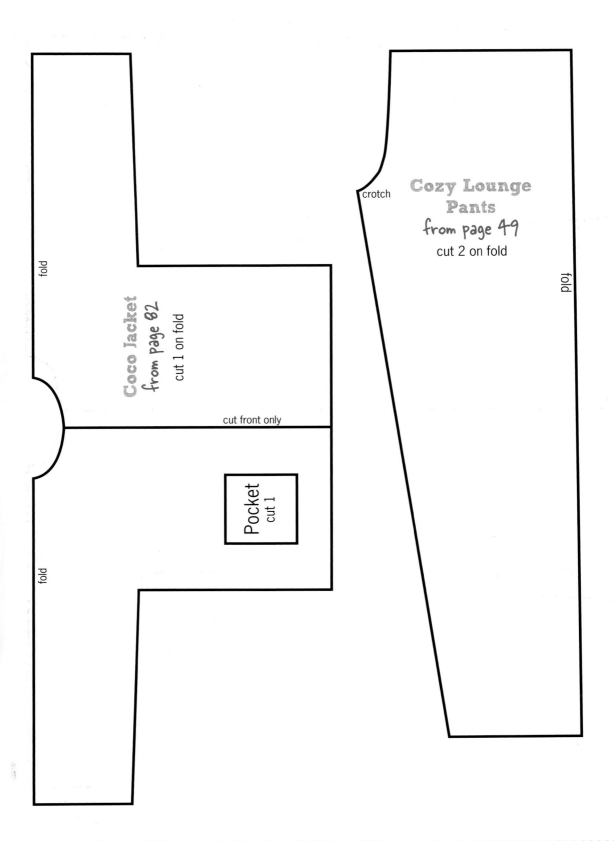

fold

Coco Jacket
from page 82
cut 1 on fold

cut front only

Pocket
cut 1

fold

crotch

Cozy Lounge
Pants
from page 49
cut 2 on fold

fold

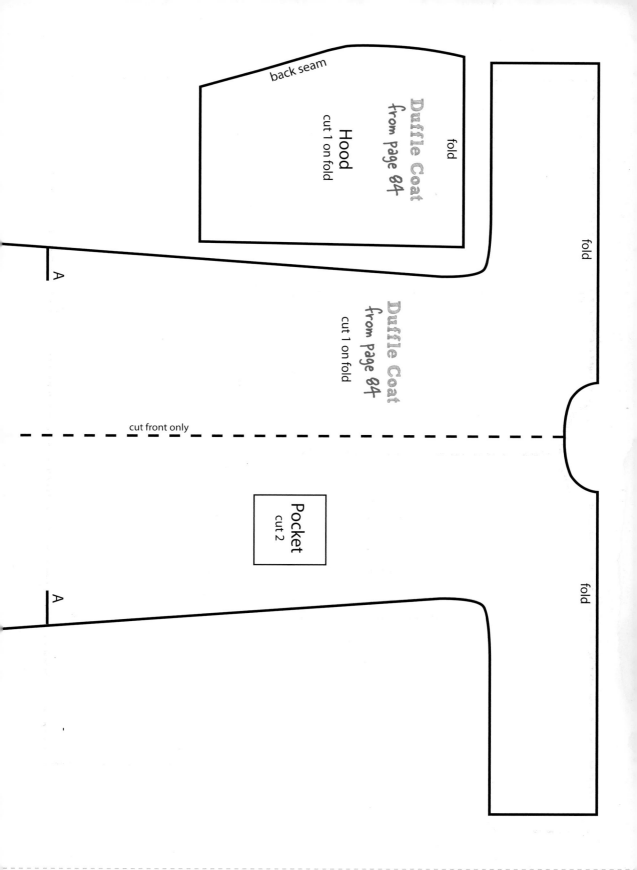

back seam

fold

Duffle Coat
from Page 84

Hood
cut 1 on fold

A

Duffle Coat
from Page 84

cut 1 on fold

fold

cut front only

Pocket
cut 2

A

fold

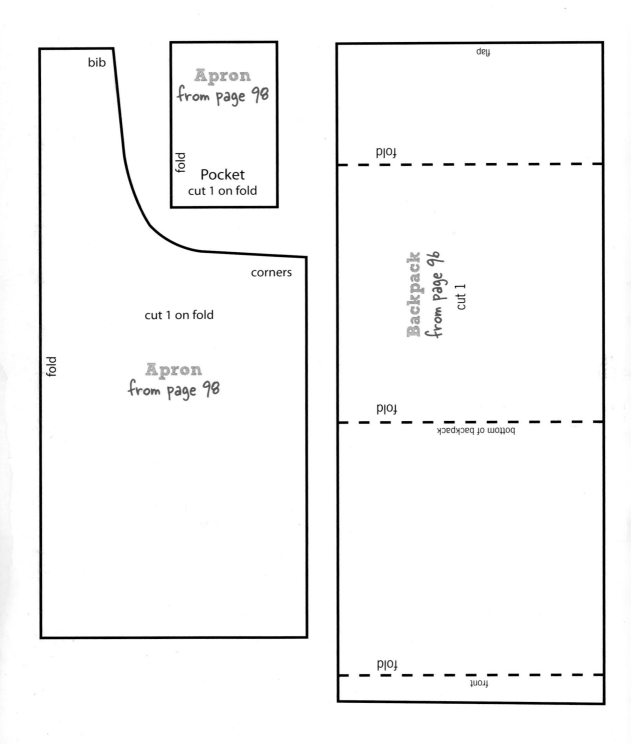

bib

Apron
from page 98

fold

Pocket
cut 1 on fold

corners

cut 1 on fold

fold

Apron
from page 98

flap

fold

Backpack
from page 96

cut 1

fold

bottom of backpack

fold

front